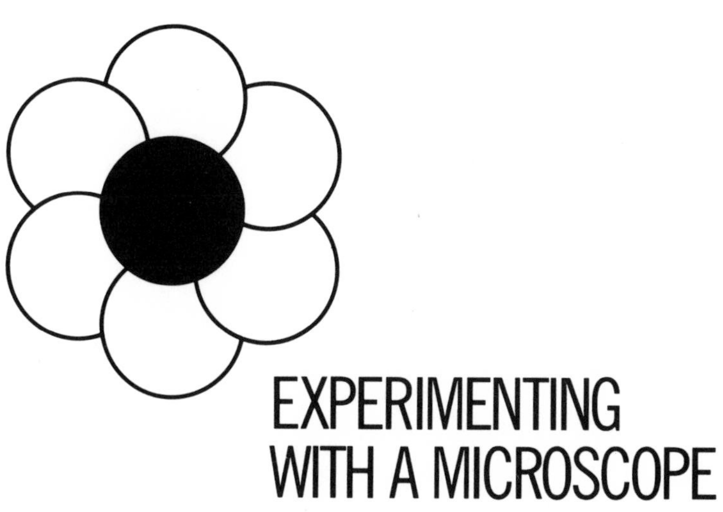

EXPERIMENTING WITH A MICROSCOPE

BY MAURICE BLEIFELD

ILLUSTRATIONS BY ANNE CANEVARI GREEN
FRANKLIN WATTS 1988
NEW YORK LONDON TORONTO SYDNEY
A VENTURE BOOK

On the cover (clockwise from top): butterfly wing scales, diatoms, plant root (*Smilax*), bread-mold (*Rhizopus*) reproduction, buttercup root tip (*Ranunculus*), and fish embryos (medaka).

Photographs courtesy of: Rijksmuseum-Stichting, Amsterdam: p. 14; AIP/Niels Bohr Library: pp. 15, 18; Trustees of The Science Museum: p. 17; Musée Pasteur: p. 21; Brookhaven National Laboratory, Photography Division, Upton, New York: p. 23; Visuals Unlimited: pp. 24 (Fred E. Hossler), 42 (top left and right) and 58 (David M. Phillips), 80 (John D. Cunningham); Carolina Biological Supply Company: pp. 42 (bottom), 82, 88, 93; R. Falk, Hebrew University, Jerusalem: p. 66.

Library of Congress Cataloging-in-Publication Data

Bleifeld, Maurice.
Experimenting with a microscope / by Maurice Bleifeld ; illustrations by Anne Canevari Green.
p. cm.—(Venture)
Bibliography: p.
Includes index.
Summary: Provides a brief history of the microscope and discusses how the microscope works, its parts, the preparation of slides, and how the microscope is used to view various specimens.
ISBN 0-531-10580-6
1. Microscope and microscopy—Juvenile literature. [1. Microscope and microscopy.] I. Green, Anne Canevari. II. Title.
QH278.B57 1988
578—dc19 88-14043 CIP AC

Printed in the United States of America
6 5 4 3 2 1

To the generation of Adam and Mica Bleifeld, Jordan and Joshua Stern, and Maxwell Kramer, who will use this book to help them explore the invisible world around them with the microscope.

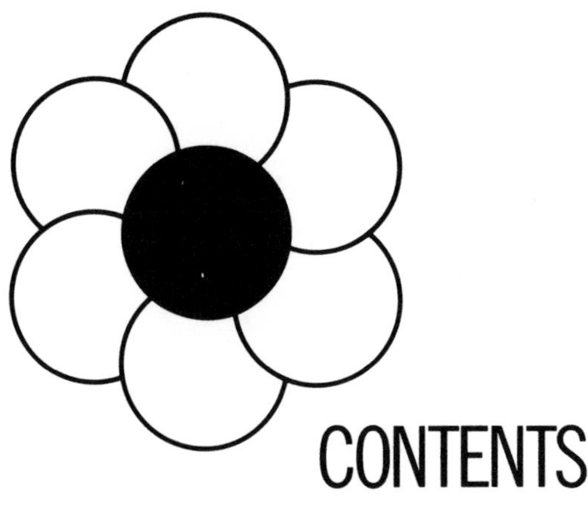

CONTENTS

THROUGH THE LOOKING GLASS • 11

CHAPTER ONE
THE MICROSCOPE THROUGH THE YEARS • 13
Leeuwenhoek. Hooke. Schleiden and Schwann. Pasteur. The Electron Microscope.

CHAPTER TWO
THE COMPOUND MICROSCOPE • 25
Parts of the Microscope. Making Slides. How to Use the Microscope. Do's and Don'ts in Using the Microscope.

CHAPTER THREE
LOOKING AT EVERYDAY OBJECTS WITH A MICROSCOPE • 39
Crystals. Hair. Textile Fibers. Snowflakes. Razor Blade. Pins and Needles.

CHAPTER FOUR
LOOKING AT PLANTS • 49
Cork Cells. Onion Cells. Green Plant Cells. Potato Starch Grains. Other Starch Grains. Pollen. Peach Skin. Other Fruit Skins. Dandelion Seed and Its Parachute. Further Ideas.

CHAPTER FIVE
LOOKING AT ANIMALS • 63
Cheek Cells. Butterfly's Wing. Eye of a Fly. Other Parts of a Fly. Beef Muscle Tissue. Voluntary Muscles. Cartilage. Fish Scales. Blood Circulation. Coffee and the Heart. A Drop of Blood. Comparing Blood Cells.

CHAPTER SIX
THE INVISIBLE WORLD • 77
Life in a Drop of Pond Water. Paramecia. Other Protozoa. Spirogyra. *Other Algae. Daphnia. Yeast. Bread Mold. Other Molds. Bacteria.*

SCIENTIFIC SUPPLY COMPANIES • 99

FOR FURTHER READING • 103

INDEX • 107

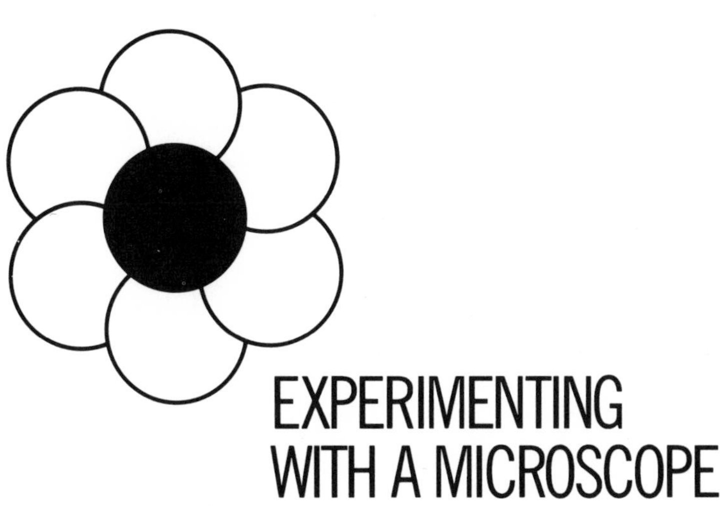

EXPERIMENTING WITH A MICROSCOPE

THROUGH THE LOOKING GLASS

An invisible world is waiting to be explored by you and your microscope. This book has been written to serve as your guide in looking at things so tiny that three hundred years ago no one even knew they existed. Imagine the excitement created when the original microscopes first revealed the wonders of an unknown world!

Let us follow in the footsteps of the early scientists who explored the newly discovered microscopic world. Start your adventures by learning how to work with a modern compound microscope. Then look through the microscope at some common objects around you. After that, the trail will take you to see what plants and animals are made of. Finally you will focus on the invisible creatures in a drop of water, creatures that live a life of their own, beyond the range of ordinary eyesight.

With a little practice and patience, you can become an expert investigator, looking through a microscope.

THE MICROSCOPE THROUGH THE YEARS

More than three hundred years ago, explorers in sailing ships were crossing the oceans to investigate the "new world" that had been discovered by Columbus. At about the same time, another type of new world—the invisible world of microscopic life—was also discovered.

LEEUWENHOEK • One of the first scientists to explore this new world was Anton van Leeuwenhoek (1632–1723), who made his great discoveries despite his lack of formal scientific training.

Van Leeuwenhoek was born in the small town of Delft, Holland, and learned a trade as a linen merchant.

Anton van Leeuwenhoek,
one of the early pioneers
of the microscope

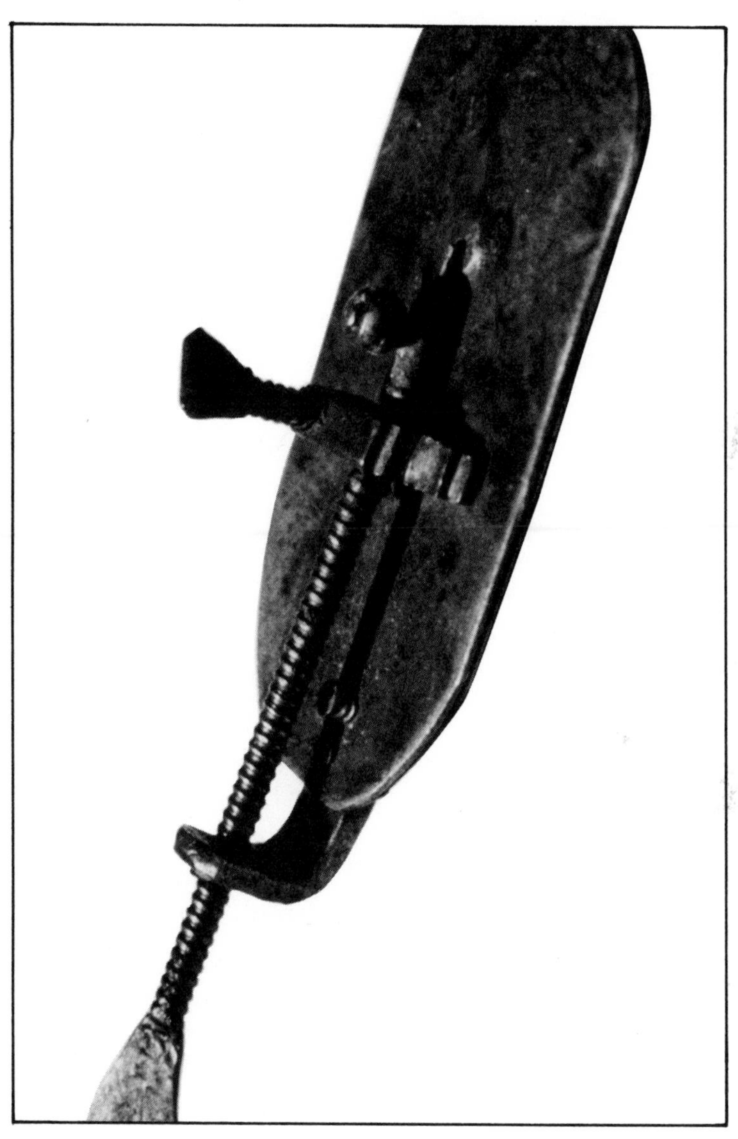

One of
van Leeuwenhoek's
microscopes

He had an unusual hobby: he liked to make tiny lenses out of glass. He would attach one of these lenses to a little opening in a metal plate. Then he would hold this simple microscope up to the light and, with the lens close to his eye, look at various specimens through it.

Leeuwenhoek had a good deal of curiosity, so he examined everything about him. He looked at a drop of pond water and was amazed to see that it contained tiny creatures moving about in their own little world. In this way, he discovered various one-celled organisms called protozoa. He also saw minute animals and algae that were barely visible to the naked eye. He found that his own red blood cells were round, and the blood cells of fish and birds were oval.

Leeuwenhoek made another remarkable discovery: bacteria. He first observed them by examining a scraping from his teeth. In a letter he wrote to the Royal Society of London, the famous scientific organization in England, he described the appearance and movement of bacteria.

Society members were so impressed that they elected him a member and invited him to keep on writing about his discoveries. He did so for fifty years, during which time he made several hundred microscopes. When he died at the age of ninety-one, people remembered him as being a skilled, careful, curious microscopist.

HOOKE • At about the same time that Leeuwenhoek was making his startling discoveries in Holland, Robert Hooke (1635–1703) was making a name for him-

Robert Hooke's microscope, shown here, more closely resembles the modern light microscope than van Leeuwenhoek's.

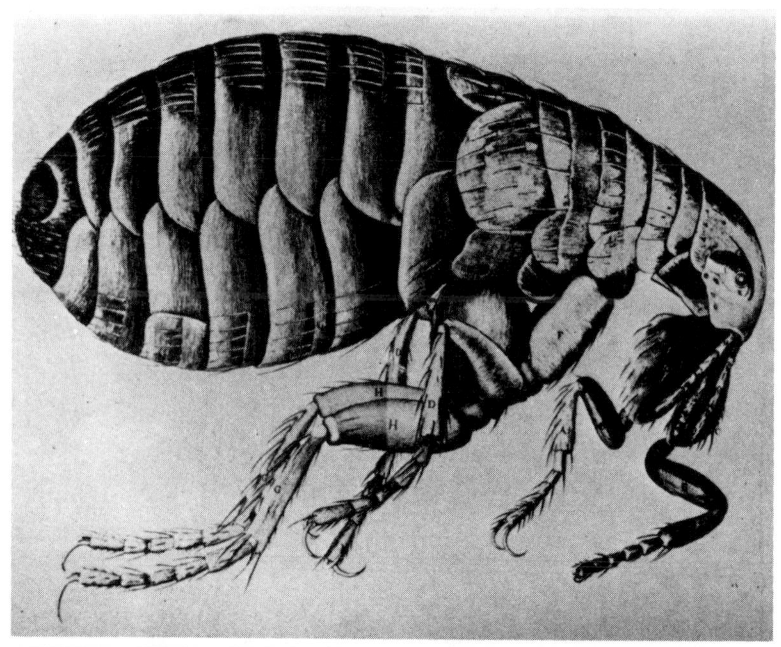

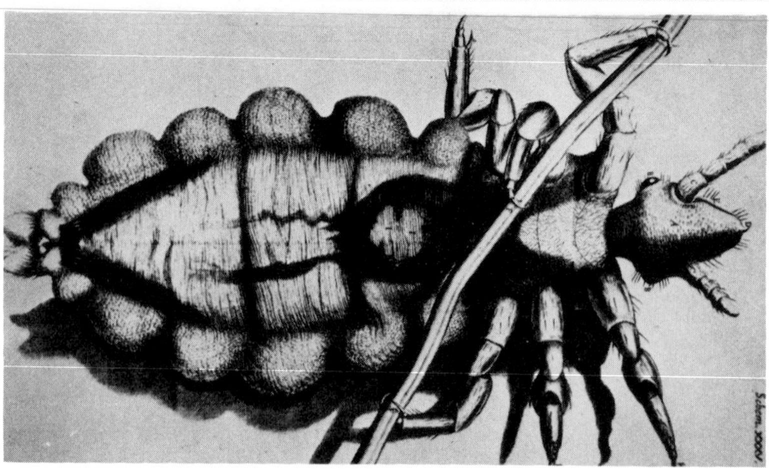

Top: Hooke's drawing of a flea;
Bottom: Hooke's drawing of a
louse holding onto a human hair.

self as one of England's most famous scientists. In his microscopy studies, he used a compound microscope, with two lenses, instead of a simple microscope like van Leeuwenhoek's. This consisted of a tube having a lens at the end near the object being examined, and another lens at the opposite end, near the eye.

Hooke made many studies of familiar objects around him and drew pictures of these objects: the point of a needle, parts of an insect, the sharp edge of a razor, organisms in rainwater, and snowflakes. In 1665, he described and illustrated his observations in *Micrographia*, the first book on the microscope ever written.

Hooke's most famous discovery with a microscope showed that cork is made of cells. When he examined a very thin slice of cork, made with "a Penknife, sharpen'd keen as a Razor," he saw that it was not solid but consisted of little boxlike cavities separated by walls. He called these cavities *cells* because they resembled little rooms.

SCHLEIDEN AND SCHWANN • Actually, Hooke did not see living cells when he examined cork under his microscope. He was only looking at the cell wall structure of empty cells; the living material had dried up long before.

As compound microscopes became more powerful, other scientists began to investigate living things with them. In 1838, one of them, Matthias Schleiden, a German botanist studying all kinds of plant tissue under the microscope, announced that all plants are made of cells. A year later, Theodor Schwann, a German zoologist who had been examining various animal tissues under the microscope, stated that all animals are made of cells.

Together, Schleiden and Schwann then announced the cell theory: All living things are made of cells. A human being and an oak tree are each made of billions of cells, all working together. There are also living things so small that they consist of only one cell, such as protozoa and algae; nevertheless, they have many parts that carry on life activities. In other words, the cell is the basic unit of life.

PASTEUR • Although Leeuwenhoek had discovered bacteria in the late seventeenth century, not until two hundred years later were some of these minute organisms shown to be a cause of disease.

One of the most famous scientists of the time, Louis Pasteur (1822–1895), used his microscope to discover bacteria that were turning wine sour and threatening the wine industry. He then heated the wine and killed these bacteria without harming the wine itself. In this way he saved the wine industry of France. In his honor, this method of preserving wine is called pasteurization.

Today, if you read the label on a container of milk, you will see that milk, too, is pasteurized. One way to pasteurize milk is to heat it to a temperature of 145°F (62.8°C) for half an hour and then cool it rapidly. This kills any harmful bacteria that may be in the milk, protecting us against diseases like tuberculosis and typhoid fever.

Louis Pasteur in his laboratory

Pasteur also showed that an animal could be helped to become immune—to protect itself against deadly bacteria. A fatal disease called anthrax was killing the herds of cattle and sheep in Europe. Under the microscope, Pasteur observed the bacteria causing anthrax. He carefully heated these bacteria enough to weaken but not kill them. Sheep injected with these weakened bacteria became slightly ill. Then they recovered and did not get anthrax at all. They had become immune.

Pasteur arranged a public demonstration to prove his discovery. In the presence of a large audience of scientists and newspaper reporters, he injected twenty-five sheep with the weakened bacteria; he kept another group of twenty-five sheep separate that were *not* injected. A few weeks later, he returned and injected all fifty sheep with a strong dose of active anthrax bacteria. A few days later, all twenty-five of the unprotected sheep were dead of anthrax. In the next field, all twenty-five of the immune sheep were running around, perfectly healthy.

This great experiment led Pasteur to develop a vaccine against rabies. Rabies is a deadly disease that is spread when an infected mammal, such as a dog (or a raccoon or a cat), bites a person or another mammal. Actually, rabies is not caused by bacteria, but by something even smaller called a virus. The rabies virus is so small that Pasteur could not even see it with his microscope. Nevertheless, he was able to weaken the virus and use it in a vaccine to save the life of a young boy in 1885.

THE ELECTRON MICROSCOPE • Although the microscope continued to be used for many years after that to study bacteria and various kinds of cells, it had one major disadvantage. It could magnify an object only up to about eighteen hundred times. It was not powerful enough to show viruses.

This problem was solved in the 1930s with the development of a new type of microscope, called the electron microscope, which can magnify objects

The electron microscope shown here illuminates a specimen by focusing electrons onto a small spot on the specimen, then scans the spot across the specimen. Signals from the specimen are then analyzed by computer to produce an image.

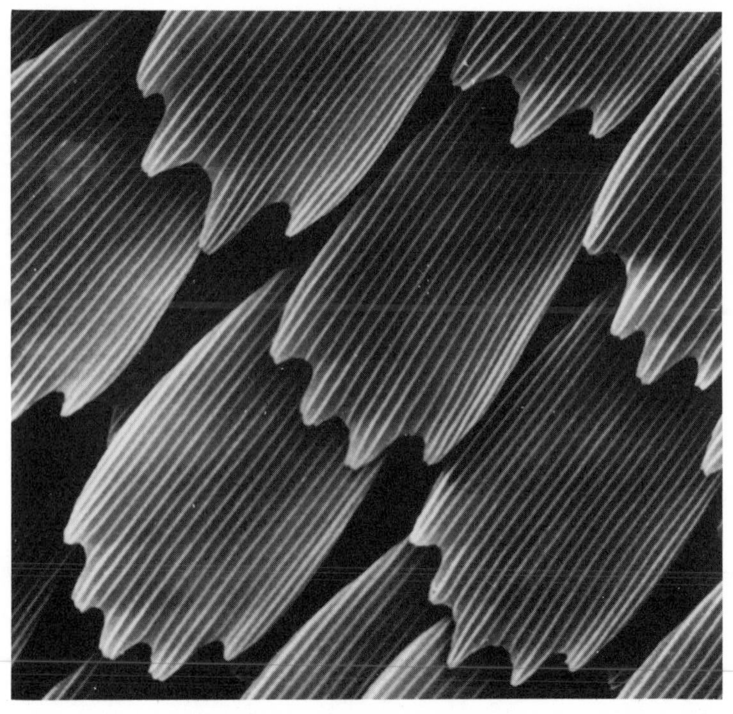

An electron-microscopic view of scales on a butterfly's wing

nearly one million times. Instead of using light, the electron microscope shoots a stream of electrons at an object. Magnets focus these electrons in the same way that lenses focus light in an ordinary microscope.

Now, viruses can be studied under the electron microscope. Also, many new types of tiny structures have been found to exist in living cells. Leeuwenhoek and Hooke would probably be astonished if they knew where their studies had led.

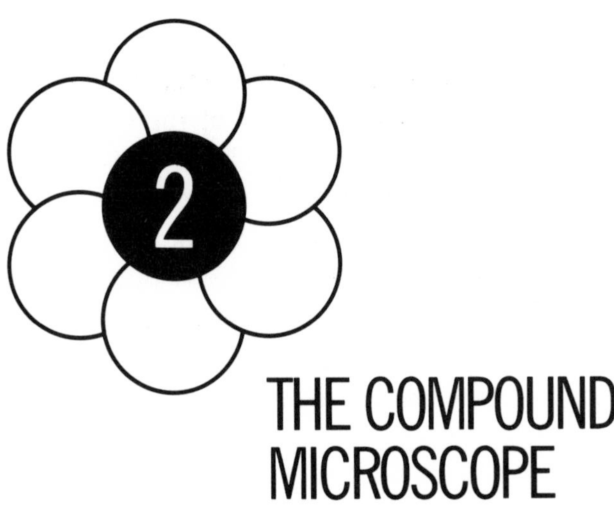

THE COMPOUND MICROSCOPE

Are you ready to look through a microscope and make your own discoveries? The microscope you use should have a good set of lenses that will give you a clear, sharp view. It is not a good idea to rely on a toy microscope because its lenses are generally inferior.

Perhaps you can arrange to use a microscope in your school. Or, you may be able to borrow one. Sometimes it is possible to buy a good used microscope. If you can afford to purchase a new one, you can order a student microscope from one of the scientific supply companies listed at the back of the book.

Now let's learn about this complicated instrument and how to use it.

PARTS OF THE MICROSCOPE • Carry the microscope to a flat desk or table by grasping the *arm* of the instrument with one hand and holding the bottom of the *base* with the other hand (Figure 1). Since the microscope is quite heavy, be careful and use both hands when you carry it. The part of the microscope you look through is called the *eyepiece*. If you look closely at the side of the eyepiece, you may be able to see it marked 10x. This means that its lenses magnify 10 times.

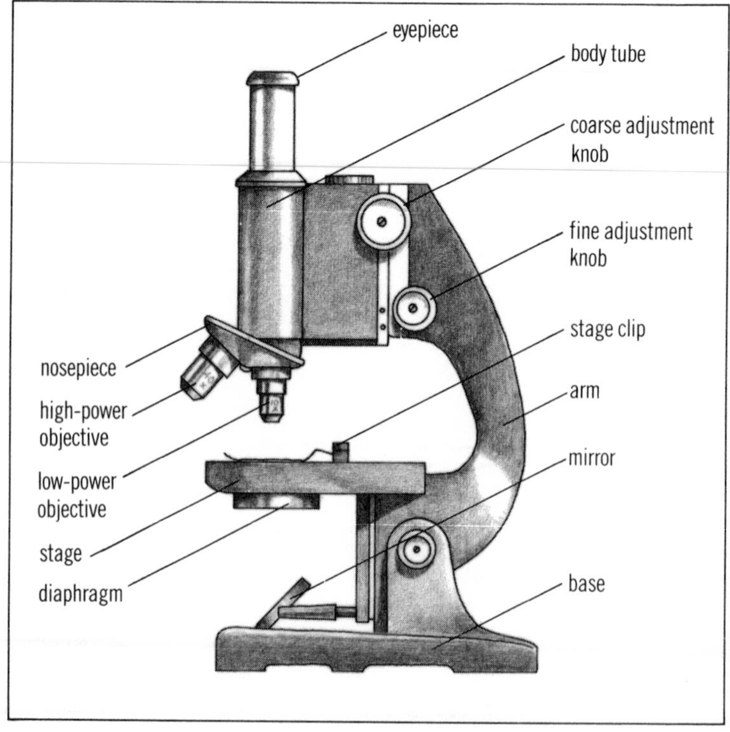

Figure 1. Parts of a compound microscope

Below is the *body tube*. You can see the *nosepiece* at its lower end. It contains two revolving *objectives*, each of which can be turned into position until it clicks. The shorter objective is the *low-power objective*; the longer one is the *high-power objective*. If you look carefully, you may see that the low-power objective is marked 10x, meaning that the lenses in it can magnify an object 10 times. The high-power objective may be marked 40x; its lenses can magnify 40 times. In some microscopes, the high-power lens has a magnification of 43x.

You may ask: What is the magnification of an object I look at under the low power? The answer is 100 times. You can figure this out by multiplying the magnifying power of the low-power objective (10x) by the amount the eyepiece magnifies (10x), for a total of 100. In the same way, you can arrive at the magnification when you use the high power—400 times (40x × 10x).

Some more-advanced microscopes have a third, *oil immersion* objective, which may be marked 100x. It provides a total magnification of 1,000 times. The word "oil" is imprinted on the objective because it dips into a special oil that concentrates the light and makes the image appear brighter. The oil immersion objective is generally used to study bacteria and other small cells.

Below the objectives is the flat *stage*, containing the *stage clips*, which hold the slide firmly in place. The center of the stage has a hole, through which light comes up from the *mirror*. Notice that the mirror can be adjusted to different positions in order to supply the best light. One side of the mirror is flat; the other has a curved surface for gathering more light. The curved side should be in place when using the high power.

Some microscopes are equipped with a *substage lamp*, which fits under the stage, in place of the mirror. When the switch is turned on, the lamp shines an even light on the specimen being examined.

Attached to the bottom of the stage is the *diaphragm*. As you use the microscope, you will learn to adjust the opening of the diaphragm and thus control the amount of light coming up from the mirror. This can help sharpen the image.

The body tube can be raised or lowered by turning the *course adjustment* knob. When you turn the *fine adjustment* knob a little in each direction, you bring the image into sharper focus.

MAKING SLIDES • Prepare a slide to practice with as you learn the steps in using the microscope. A good object for this purpose is the letter *e* from a newspaper. With a pair of scissors, cut out a small square of the paper with the *e* in the middle.

Use tweezers to place the *e* in the center of a glass slide. Add a drop of water from a medicine dropper to cover the square of paper. Carefully place a cover slip over the square paper in this way: Lower one side of the cover slip so that it touches the slide at an angle, just at the edge of the drop of water (Figure 2A). Now gently lower the other end of the cover slip over the drop of water (Figure 2B) until the cover slip completely covers the water (Figure 2C).

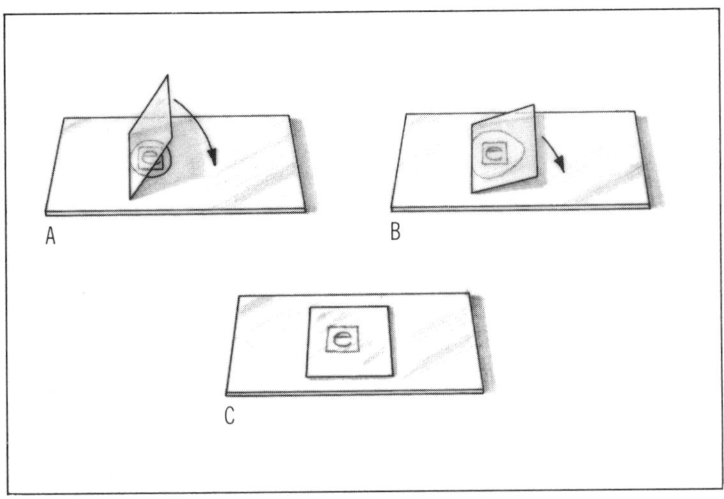

Figure 2. Placing a cover slip on a slide

If, instead of doing it this way, you just drop the cover slip on the water, you may find that you have trapped some air bubbles under it. These air bubbles will interfere with your view of the specimen. If air bubbles do appear on the slide, try to move them away by gently tapping the cover slip with the rubber bulb of the medicine dropper.

You have just prepared a temporary slide. Many other specimens can also be examined with a slide made in this way. The slide is considered temporary because after a while the water will evaporate. You can add more water without removing the cover slip by placing the end of a medicine dropper alongside the cover slip. Slowly squeeze out a drop of water and watch it spread under the cover slip (Figure 3).

Figure 3. Adding more water under the cover slip

When you are finished with a slide, you can clean it in warm water containing a drop of dish detergent. Hold the slide by its sides and rinse it under the faucet. To dry it, stand it up at an angle on a dry paper towel, letting its upper end rest against a small jar. This allows the water to drain off without leaving any marks on the slide. Cover slips can be cleaned the same way. But since they are very thin and break easily, handle them carefully. Hold them by their sides so you do not leave finger marks on them.

To prepare a permanent slide, follow the same method, but instead of water, you need a special liquid called Canada balsam. This liquid is clear and will harden in about two weeks. However, if the specimen is not completely dry, the Canada balsam will turn cloudy. Canada balsam can be purchased from the scientific supply companies listed at the end of this book. Have your parents or a teacher help you do this.

Place a drop of Canada balsam directly on a dry square newsprint with the *e*. Carefully lower a cover slip over it, without trapping any air bubbles. Put it aside in a flat position. In about two weeks you will find that the cover slip has become cemented to the slide, with the *e* in between. The slide can now be stored vertically in a special slide box as part of your permanent collection.

SAFETY

When preparing specimens for observation on slides, have an adult do the cutting or slicing if you feel uncomfortable using a razor blade or knife. If you do the cutting or slicing yourself, work under adult supervision and be very careful not to cut yourself. Use a single-edge razor blade in a holder whenever possible. You can also try using a hobby knife.
If you do cut yourself, wash the cut thoroughly with soap and water and use a disinfectant. Clean your tools when you are through with them and store them out of reach of any younger children who might be around your work area.

Prepare permanent slides of other dry specmens, such as human hair, the "dust" from a butterfly's wing, the wing of a fly, cotton thread, wool fiber, or nylon thread.

HOW TO BUILD A SLIDE BOX

1. Draw the pattern shown in Figure 4A on a firm piece of cardboard, leaving enough room at the bottom of the box for the length of a slide.

2. The sides of the box should be a little higher than the width of a slide.

3. Fold along the dotted lines to form a box; hold the slides in place with strips of masking tape.

4. Attach paper clips along the length of the box, on each side, leaving enough room between the clips for the thickness of a slide.

5. Draw the pattern shown in Figure 4B on a piece of cardboard and fold along the dotted lines in the shape of a cover.

6. Attach the bottom part of the cover to the back of the box with strips of masking tape. Now the slide box, Figure 4C, is ready.

HOW TO USE THE MICROSCOPE • Are you now ready to learn how to use the microscope? First you will learn to use the low power and then the high power. Use the letter *e* slide for both activities until you feel ready to go on to other specimens. Always start with low power, never with high.

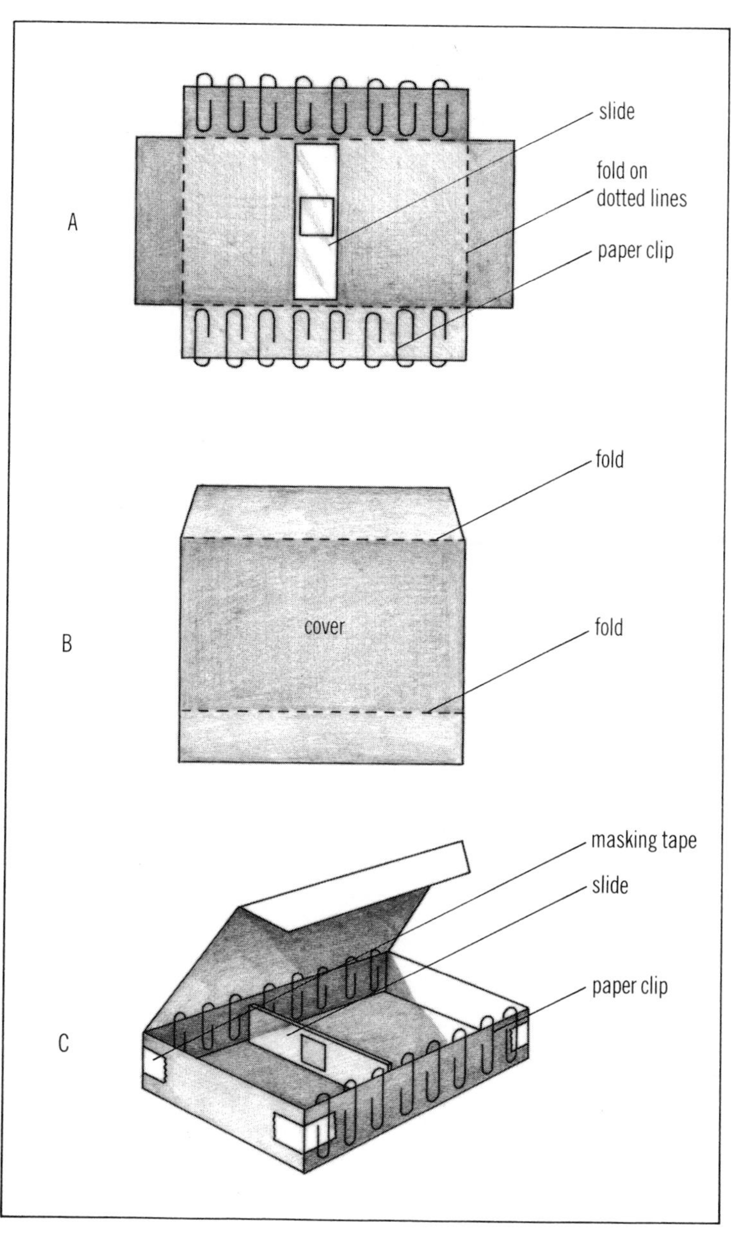

Figure 4. How to build a slide box

To use the low power, follow these steps:

1. Place the microscope on a flat table where you can obtain a good light. During the day, the sky is the best source of light, but the sun will give a distorted image. (CAUTION: NEVER PUT THE MICROSCOPE IN DIRECT SUNLIGHT. IT IS TOO BRIGHT AND CAN HARM YOUR EYES.) As you look through the microscope, move the curved mirror into the position that will give you the best possible light.

2. Place the slide on the stage and keep it in place with the stage clips. The *e* should be directly over the center of the opening in the stage.

3. Turn the low-power objective until it clicks into place.

4. With your eye at the level of the stage so that you can watch the bottom of the low-power objective, turn the coarse adjustment knob and lower the objective until it is about a quarter of an inch (7 millimeters) from the slide. The reason for watching the bottom of the objective is that you do not want it to smash into the slide. This accident could happen if you were looking through the eyepiece while lowering the objective. There is also the possibility that you could scratch the lens of the objective. Never lower the objective with the coarse adjustment while you are looking through the eyepiece.

5. Now look through the eyepiece and gradually *raise* the objective until the image comes into view. Move the coarse adjustment knob a little in either direction to get a sharper view of the image.

6. Shift your fingers to the fine adjustment knob and rotate it a little for an even sharper view.

7. Place your fingers under the stage and move the diaphragm back and forth until the image is as clear as possible. Sometimes, by cutting down on the light a bit, you can see details that were not visible because the light was too bright.

8. As you study the *e*, you can make several observations: The *e* is very large and practically fills the field of vision; the *e* itself is not solid—the patches of printer's ink seem broken up as they come in contact with the different parts of the rough paper. Notice that the *e* is upside down and backward. This tells you something about the effect of the lenses on an image—the image is reversed.

9. More observations: While looking through the microscope, slowly move the slide to the right. Do you observe that the image of the slide moves to the left? Move the slide back to the left. Does the image now move to the right? Gently move the slide toward you. Can you see the image move away from you? Now move the slide away from you and watch the image move in the opposite direction.

To use the high power, follow *these* steps:

1. While the low power is as clear as possible, turn the high-power objective into position until it clicks into place. Notice how close the bottom of the objective is to the slide. Because of this, you will understand why you should only use the fine adjustment when viewing a specimen with the high power.

2. Rotate the fine adjustment knob a little in either direction until the image appears sharp and clear.

3. Open the diaphragm a little to admit more light.

4. Keep your fingers lightly on the fine adjustment knob as you look through the high power. Continue turning it slowly in either direction, to make new observations. At this high magnification, it may be hard for you to realize that the broken, black splotches you are looking at are part of the letter *e*. Notice how the newspaper itself consists of many fibers.

DO'S AND DON'TS IN USING THE MICROSCOPE • 1. Try to keep both eyes open as you look through the eyepiece. With a little practice, you will find that it is more relaxing and less of a strain on your eyes.

2. Do not always use the same eye when looking through the microscope. Use the other eye, also, to give the first eye a rest.

3. Use special lens paper to lightly clean the lenses. Do not use a handkerchief, facial tissue, or anything else, or you may scratch the lenses.

4. Do not touch the lenses with your fingers. The oils in your skin may be left behind on the lenses.

5. When not using the microscope, keep it covered in a safe place.

6. If you wear glasses, take them off when you look through the microscope. Otherwise, the glasses may become scratched by the metal of the eyepiece.

7. When you hold a slide or a cover slip, place your thumb and pointing finger along the sides. If you touch the slide's or cover slip's surface with your fingers, you will leave oil marks from your skin.

8. Although you may want to examine a slide under high power, always start by first looking at it under low power; then, when you have focused sharply on the object, switch to high power. In other words, do not use high power first; the high-power objective is too close to the slide and may break it.

3

LOOKING AT EVERYDAY OBJECTS WITH A MICROSCOPE

Now that you know how to use the microscope properly, look at some common objects around you.

CRYSTALS • Crystals are always fun and interesting to observe. Described below are just a few of the substances you can explore.

SALT ○ Put a pinch of salt on a slide and examine it under low power. This is a dry preparation and does not require a drop of water or a cover slip. Adjust the mirror and the diaphragm for the best possible view. What shape are the salt crystals? Notice how the light glances off them.

Do they remind you of anything you might find in your refrigerator or freezer?

While looking through the eyepiece, move the mirror to shine different amounts of light through the salt. Insert a piece of black paper under the slide and shine a flashlight down on top of the slide. How do the crystals look now, against a dark background? Also try shining the light from the side. Do you see the crystals sparkle as they pick up the light from different angles?

To see how salt dissolves in water, place a cover slip over the salt. Touch a medicine dropper containing water to the edge of the cover slip (not on top of it) and release a drop of water. Watch the water spread under the cover slip. Now quickly look at the salt crystals under the microscope. Before your eyes, they will shrink in size as they come in contact with the water, and then disappear altogether. The water is now a salt solution.

Set the slide aside for a few hours and let the water under the cover slip dry up. When you examine it under the low power, can you see salt crystals again? Do they still have the same shape?

SUGAR AND SAND ○ Look at some sugar under low power. Compare its crystals with those of salt. Then examine the effect of adding a drop of water in the same way as you did with the salt crystals. Do the sugar crystals also disappear as they dissolve? Also look at grains of sand. Are they all the same size and shape?

HAIR ● It's time you looked at a hair from your head. Snip off a small piece from the end of a hair, place it on a slide, and add a drop of water and a cover slip. Focus under low power and high power. Adjust the diaphragm for the best light.

Do you notice how smooth the hair is? This part of the hair, called the *shaft*, is not living. Along the center of the shaft, you may be able to see the small collections of dark pigment that give hair its color. Now look at the other end of the hair, the part contained in your scalp. Pull one strand of hair out (are you ready to make this sacrifice for the sake of science?) and snip off about ½ inch (13 millimeters) of the bottom part.

Notice that it appears to consist of a tiny swelling at its end. This is the *follicle*, the growing part of the hair. Place the follicle on a slide and cover it with a drop of water, then a cover slip. Examine it under both low power and high power. Notice how different it looks from the rest of the hair. It contains many living cells that keep on producing the shaft.

Look at different-colored hair: black, brown, red, blond, gray, and white. Compare these with one another. Look at straight hair, wavy hair, and kinky hair. Also look at hair from a dog, cat, or any other animal and compare it with human hair.

TEXTILE FIBERS • Now look at your clothing under the microscope. The cloth is made of textile fibers that may consist of cotton, wool, silk, polyester, or other materials. Look at a small piece of cloth under the low power and observe the cross-weaving pattern.

COTTON ○ A good way to see what cotton fiber looks like is to take a short length of white cotton thread

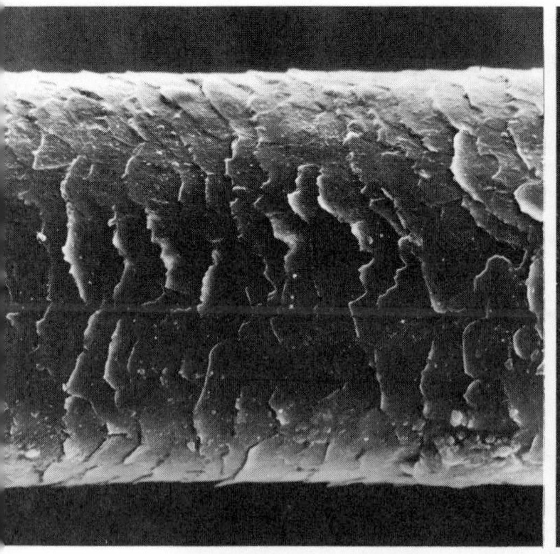

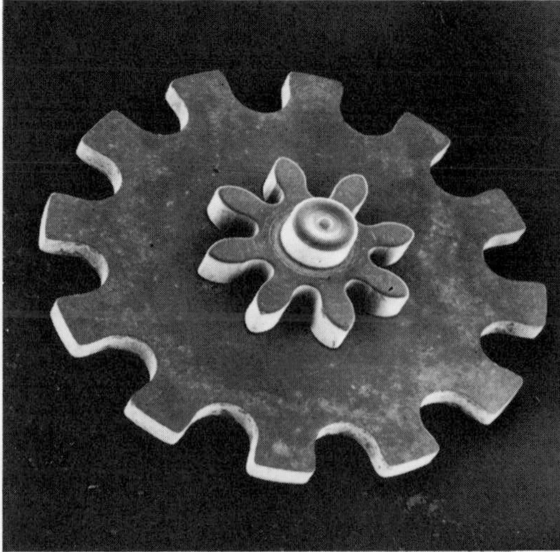

Do these magnified objects resemble anything you have viewed under the microscope? If not, what do you think they are? Check your guess using a microscope. Then look at the answers below.

A. Human hair. B. Watch part. C. Beach sand.

from a spool. Read the label to make sure it is cotton. Hold the cotton thread down on the slide with tweezers in one hand. With your other hand use a pin to spread the cotton apart into its fibers.

When you can see the individual fibers, add a drop of water and a cover slip. Under low power, a cotton fiber looks like a long, clear, twisted tube. Under high power, use the fine adjustment to bring the fiber into sharp focus. What do you see now?

Move the fine adjustment knob slightly back and forth in order to follow the texture of the fiber (Figure 5A).

Cotton fibers come from the flower of the cotton plant that has developed into a white fluffy mass called the boll. After the cotton bolls are picked, these fibers are drawn out into cotton threads, for use in making cloth and in sewing.

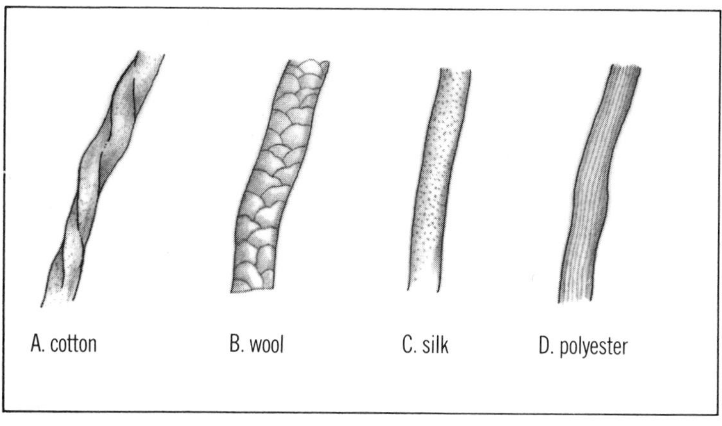

Figure 5. Textile fibers

WOOL ○ By comparison, the wool in your sweater comes from an animal—sheep. Obtain a small strand of wool from a ball of wool or from a piece of woolen clothing. Place it on a slide and spread it apart as much as you can with two needles. Then add a drop of water and a cover slip.

Under low power, the wool fibers look like long, narrow tubes with fine lines across them from side to side. Switch to high power and, if necessary, use the diaphragm to cut down on the light a little. Use the fine adjustment knob to see that the wool fiber is covered with scales (Figure 5B). For a clearer view of these scales, turn the mirror aside and shine a flashlight down on the slide from the side. Compare wool fibers from different articles of clothing. Are there any differences?

SILK ○ You may know that we obtain silk from the silkworm, which is not a worm at all. It is really the caterpillar stage of a large moth. After it has reached a certain size in its growth, the caterpillar spins threads of silk to form a bulky cocoon about 2 inches long and ½ inch (50 millimeters by 13 millimeters) wide. The silk of the cocoon can be drawn out by a special method and spun into a long thread hundreds of feet long. It is then used to make fine silk cloth.

Look in your house for a pure silk tie or silk dress and, *with a parent's permission*, carefully snip a few threads of silk from an unimportant seam. Spread them out on a slide with two needles. Add a drop of water and a cover slip. What do you see under low power? What do you see under high power (Figure 5C)?

POLYESTER ○ Unlike cotton, wool, and silk, which are produced by living things, polyester is made from chemicals in a factory. We call it a synthetic material.

Snip away a small thread from an unimportant seam of a polyester shirt or other article made of polyester. Place it on a slide, spread it apart with needles, and add a drop of water and a cover slip.

Notice how the fibers are long, straight, and smooth. They take this appearance when a liquid solution comes out of a device having tiny holes, called *spinnerettes*, and hardens into fine synthetic threads. Under high power, you can see how even they are (Figure 5D). They resemble silk in appearance, but they do not contain the tiny grains you saw in silk.

OTHER TEXTILES ○ Collect different types of textiles containing rayon, linen, nylon, dacron, etc., and examine their appearance under the microscope. Study the weave of a piece of their cloth. Make a permanent slide of each type of thread, label it, and add it to your collection. Now that you know what the various fibers look like under the microscope, can you play the part of a detective and identify the makeup of an unknown piece of fabric?

SNOWFLAKES • In the wintertime, while it is snowing, you may be able to see the special structure of a snowflake. Cut a piece of black construction paper or a piece of dull black cloth, like velvet, the size of a slide. Put it in the freezer or outside for about half an hour, so it will be cold enough to keep the snowflake from melting.

Place your microscope close to an open window, let some snow fall on the cold paper, and put the black paper containing the snow under low power. Do not use a cover slip. As you focus on the snowflake, you may want to shine a flashlight down on the stage for the best light. Some of the snowflakes may appear as crystals with six sides. Seen against the black background, they have a beautiful appearance.

You may have read somewhere that no two snowflakes look alike. Each six-sided crystal is supposed to have its own individual shape. Study different snowflakes and make a simple drawing of their shapes. Are they all different?

RAZOR BLADE • Place a new razor blade on the stage of the microscope so that the sharp edge lies across the opening. (CAUTION: BE CAREFUL NOT TO CUT YOURSELF.) Look at it under the low power. Do you see the clean, straight line that the sharp edge has? Now switch to high power. Does the edge still look like a straight line? Do you see any small indentations here and there?

Compare the new blade with an old, used razor blade. Can you see why it is no longer sharp? Even though the edge still looks like a straight line to the naked eye, can you see many indentations under low power? Under high power?

PINS AND NEEDLES • Place the point of a pin across the opening of the stage. Inspect it under both low and high power. How sharp does the pin look? Now, do the same with the point of a small needle. How does its point compare with that of a pin? Look at the eye of the needle and notice the width of its space. Examine a large needle and compare its point with that of the small needle.

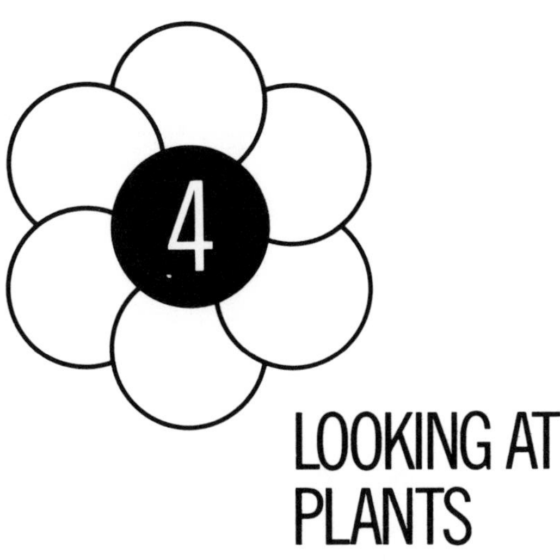

LOOKING AT PLANTS

What are plants made of? It is easy to use the microscope to see inside of them and observe their cells.

CORK CELLS • Follow in the footsteps of Robert Hooke, who first gave us the name "cell" when he looked at the boxlike structures of cork with his microscope over three hundred years ago.

Use a sharp, single-edge razor blade or hobby knife to cut off a very thin slice from a cork. Under low power, you should be able to see rows of small, boxlike cells. If your slice is thin enough, you can get a better view of the individual cork cells under high power.

However, cork consists only of the cell-wall structures of empty cells. To see the living parts of a cell, go on to the next activity.

CAUTION: BE CAREFUL IN HANDLING THE BLADE OR KNIFE AND WORK UNDER ADULT SUPERVISION. IF YOU ARE NOT SURE ABOUT DOING THIS ACTIVITY YOURSELF, ASK A GROWN-UP TO DO IT FOR YOU.

ONION CELLS • One of the simplest ways of seeing living cells is to use an ordinary onion. Cut away a quarter of a raw onion and use your fingers to peel away one of its sections. Notice the clear white surface of the thin membrane covering it. This onion skin is only a single layer of cells thick. Use a sharp knife or scalpel to cut ¼-inch (7-millimeter) squares into the onion skin and partly into the fleshy tissue under it. Grip the corner of one of these squares with tweezers and lift off the square of onion skin (Figure 6A).

Place the square on a slide. Cover it with a drop of iodine solution and a cover slip. You can make up some iodine solution by placing 2 drops of tincture of iodine from your medicine chest in a small jar and adding 30 drops of water. (CAUTION: NEVER PUT TINCTURE OF IODINE IN YOUR MOUTH.) This yellowish-brown iodine solution serves as a stain to dye parts of the cell and make them more visible. Another stain you can use is blue-ink solution. Prepare it by putting 2 drops of blue ink in a small jar and adding 10 drops of water.

Examine the slide under low power.

Do you notice how the cells are arranged like

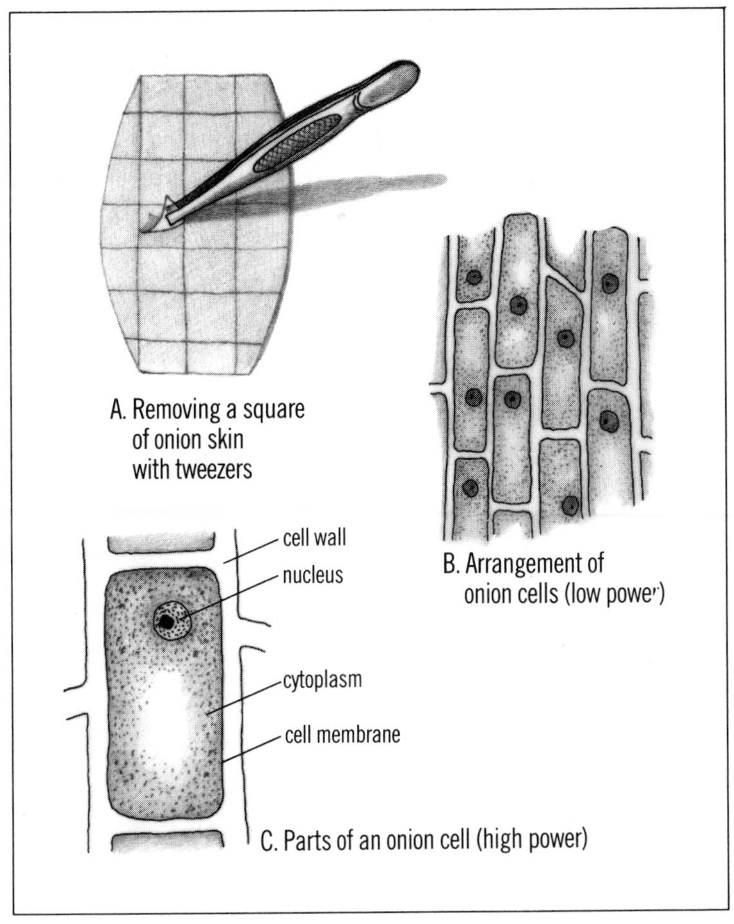

Figure 6. Examining onion cells

bricks in a wall (Figure 6B)? Each cell has a regular shape because it is supported by its firm *cell wall*. Look for the round, dense spot in each cell. This is the *nucleus*. It controls the activities of the cell.

If you close the diaphragm of the microscope so that the light is less bright, you should be able to make out the liquid part which fills the cell. This part is the *cytoplasm*. It seems to be made of tiny granules. Look for these granules under high power (Figure 6c). The cytoplasm carries on the life activities of the cell. Covering the outside of the cytoplasm is the *cell membrane*, which controls the movement of substances into and out of the cell.

STAINS ○ Iodine solution and blue-ink solution are only two of many stains that can be used to dye the parts of onion cells. Try a drop of red-ink solution on a fresh piece of onion skin and compare the appearance of the cells. People who study cells use a variety of stains, for example: methylene blue, neutral red, and gentian violet. Perhaps your teacher or another knowledgeable adult can help you obtain these from a scientific supply company or school science department.

GREEN PLANT CELLS • Leaves are green because they contain *chloroplasts*, little green structures where food is made using light. Since the leaf of a tree is too thick to examine with a microscope, we turn to a small plant called *elodea* that grows in ponds and is often used in aquariums. Elodea is only two cells thick and can easily be studied.

You can usually obtain elodea in a pet shop that sells tropical fish. It may be sold there by another name, *anacharis*. Remove one of the small leaves and place it on a slide. Add a drop of water and a cover slip. Under low power, you can see the even rows of cells.

Turn the fine adjustment knob slowly. How many layers of cells can you see? Switch to high power and keep using the fine adjustment until you can see the cells clearly. Notice the little green oval bodies along the outer part of a cell. These are the chloroplasts (Figure 7). They are located within the cytoplasm.

You should be able to see an interesting thing happen. The chloroplasts will be moving around the inner wall of a cell, along its length and then around the side to the other side. They are actively being carried along by the cytoplasm, which streams around the cell. If they are not moving, you may be able to get them started by warming the slide on the palm of your hand for about a minute. If they still don't move, try another leaf from the tip of the stem.

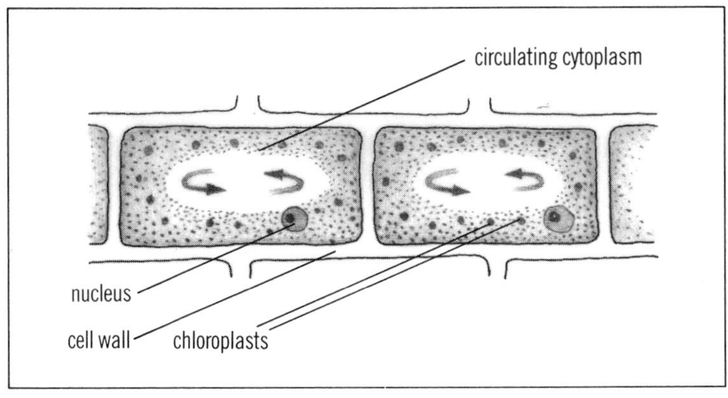

Figure 7. Cells of an elodea leaf

Try to figure out the best way to get the chloroplasts streaming around the cell. *Hint*: Leave the slide in sunlight for a minute. If that doesn't work, try it for two minutes. *Another method*: Use a drop of warm water when you first make the slide. Would a thermometer be helpful?

POTATO STARCH GRAINS • Peel away part of the skin of a potato. CAREFULLY use a sharp razor blade or knife to make a very thin slice of the potato. Place it on a slide; add a drop of water and a cover slip. Under low power, focus on the thinnest edge of the slice. The cells are large. Are they shaped regularly or irregularly? Do you see small, pearly-white starch grains inside the cells?

Study the cells and the starch grains under high power (Figure 8A). Observe the varying shapes and sizes of the starch grains. Do you know that iodine solution can be used to test for the presence of starch? To prove this, place a drop of tincture of iodine on a small piece of potato. What happens?

The presence of the color shows that starch is present. Try the test with a piece of bread.

Now let's see how starch grains are affected by iodine. Add a drop of iodine solution to the side (not the top) of the cover slip. Place a small piece of paper towel alongside the other side of the cover slip (Figure 8B). The paper acts like a sponge and soaks up the iodine solution under the cover slip. As the iodine solution is being absorbed by the paper towel, the drop of iodine solution is moving under the cover slip to take its place.

What happens after a few minutes?

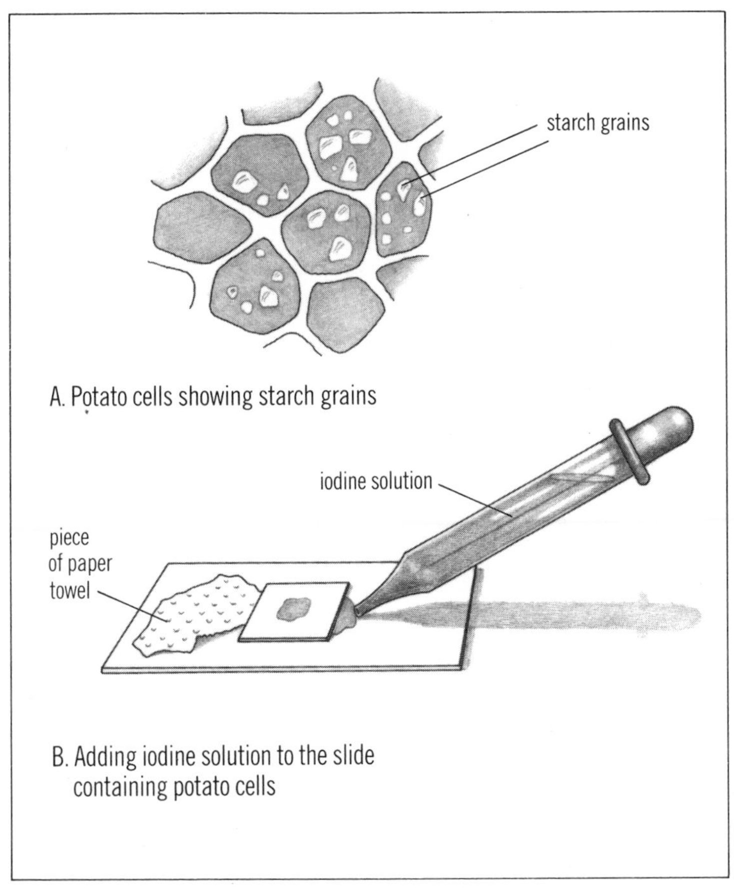

Figure 8. Studying potato starch grains

OTHER STARCH GRAINS • If you have no corn starch in your kitchen, buy a small container of it in a grocery store. Prepare a slide with a pinch of the starch in a drop of water. Observe the starch grains under low and high power. Compare their size and shape with potato starch grains. Observe the effect of iodine solution on the corn starch grains. Do they turn blue? Also try arrowroot starch, wheat starch, tapioca, or any other available starch. Use the microscope to compare the size and shape of these starch grains with those of potato and corn.

POLLEN • If you look closely at a flower, you will notice some yellow powder. This powdery substance is pollen. Pollen is very important in the steps of making the seeds of a flower.

Shake some of the pollen from a flower onto a slide. Add a drop of water and a cover slip. Under low power, you can see the numerous tiny pollen grains. Switch to high power for a more detailed view. What shape are the pollen grains? Do any of them have little spines all over them (Figure 9A)?

When pollen normally lands on a flower, it sprouts a pollen tube that grows down into the plant, to begin the formation of the seeds. You can get pollen grains to sprout tubes on a slide by using a sugar solution. A special slide called a depression slide is used for this purpose.

With the blunt end of a toothpick, spread some petroleum jelly lightly around the depression. Sprinkle some pollen over the center of a cover slip. Prepare a sugar solution by adding a teaspoon of sugar to half a glass of water. Add a drop of the solution to the pollen and turn the cover slip over quickly, so that the drop does not spread. Carefully place the cover slip on the slide, with the drop hanging freely over the depression. Press the sides of the slip gently, using a pencil eraser to form a seal with the petroleum jelly (Figure 9B).

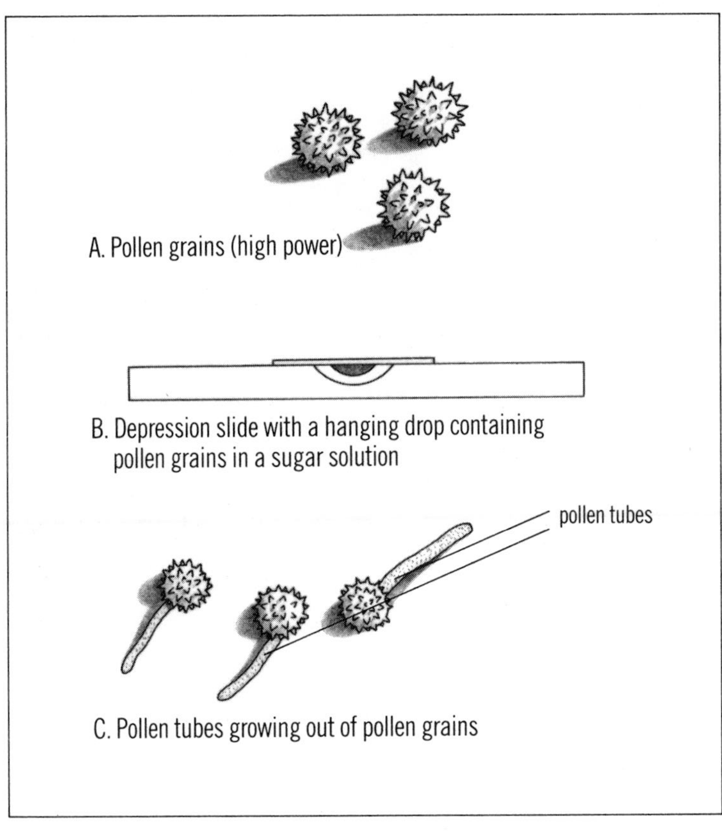

Figure 9. Pollen grains of a cosmos flower

Set the slide aside for at least 30 minutes. Look under low power to see whether any of the pollen grains have begun to sprout tubes. If nothing has happened, take a look every 10 minutes. If you are patient, you should be able to see the pollen tubes (Figure 9C).

Make a study of pollen from different flowers. You can collect the pollen in small, separate enve-

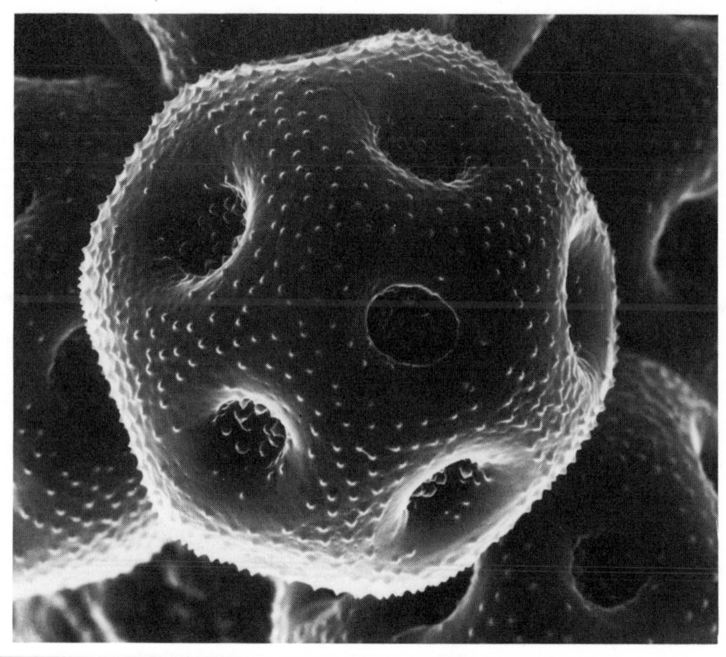

A pollen grain, magnified 13,000 times by an electron microscope

lopes. Prepare slides and examine under low and high power. Compare the size and shape of the various pollen grains. Do you see tiny hooks or other special structures attached to some types? What shape are they?

Prepare permanent slides of different pollen grains, by adding a drop of Canada balsam and a cover slip. Find out the best type of sugar solution for growing pollen tubes, by using more or less sugar in preparing the sugar solution.

PEACH SKIN • When you hold a peach, have you noticed that it has a fuzzy skin? Let's look at the skin to see what makes it fuzzy. With a sharp razor blade or knife (BE CAREFUL!) cut a very thin slice off the skin and place it on a slide. Add a drop of water and a cover slip.

What do you see under low power? Rotate the fine adjustment knob slowly in each direction so that you can see different parts of the object.

Carefully use the point of a knife to gently rub some of the fuzz off the skin onto a slide; add a drop of water and a cover slip. Locate some of the hairlike projections under low power and then switch to high power. Study the individual hairs (Figure 10).

OTHER FRUIT SKINS • Compare the fuzzy skin of a peach with that of an apricot. Under low power, what does

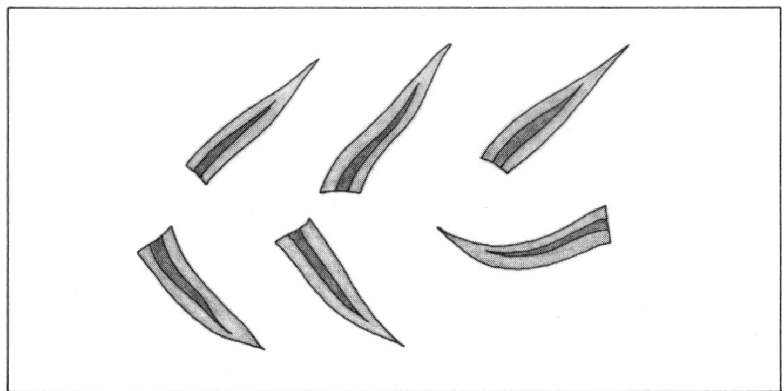

Figure 10. Hairlike projections on the skin of a peach

a thin slice of apricot show? Use high power. Compare what you see with what you saw on a peach. Now examine a nectarine. Would you expect to find hairs on its skin? Study a thin slice of the skin under the microscope and discover the answer for yourself. Check the skin of other fuzzy and smooth fruits.

DANDELION SEED AND ITS PARACHUTE • Have you ever looked at a dandelion plant on a lawn and noticed the round, white delicate structure at the end of the stem? The flower is so light and fluffy, it seems to be made of cobwebs. Then, if you blow into it, the cobwebs seem to vanish as the dainty parts drift away in the breeze.

Try to find one of these plants. Before you blow it apart, pick one of the fine sections with tweezers and detach it from the rest of the round formation. Can you see that there is a small dark seed at one end and a fine stem which ends in a collection of many small white hairs sticking out from it? This white part attached to the seed is called the parachute. The slightest breeze scatters the seeds to different places where they will develop into new plants.

Carefully place some of these seeds with their attached parachutes into a small envelope and take them home. Put one on a slide; add a drop of water and a cover slip. Look at it under low power. First examine the seed. Do you see many small hooks? They help hold the seed down on the ground when it lands (Figure 11).

Look at the fine white hairlike structures of the parachute. Are there a lot of them? Focus on one

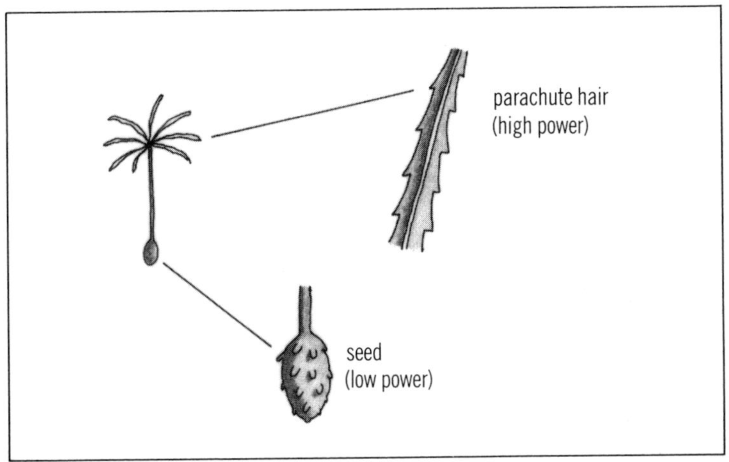

Figure 11. Dandelion seed and its parachute hair

under high power to study it. What do you notice along its length?

FURTHER IDEAS • Find a dandelion plant with its light seedball. Using tweezers, gently pick it apart, one seed at a time. How many seeds are there altogether? How are the parachutes arranged next to one another in the seedball? The milkweed plant also produces seeds with parachutes. Make a microscopic study of a milkweed seed parachute. Use Canada balsam to prepare permanent slides of these seeds and their parachutes.

LOOKING AT ANIMALS

Just as the microscope enables you to see what plants are made of, it can also be used to examine animals. A good place to begin is with cells from your own body.

CHEEK CELLS • You can easily obtain cells from your own body by using a flat toothpick. Scrape the inside of your cheek *lightly* with the blunt end. Spread the wet material gently on a slide. If you apply too much pressure in doing this, you may damage and distort the cells. Add a drop of stain such as blue-ink solution or iodine solution and cover with a cover slip.

Under low power, you will see collections of small cells. It may be

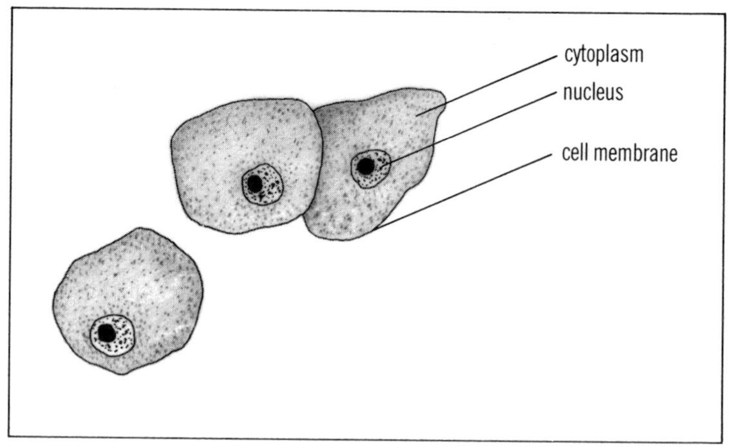

Figure 12. Cheek cells

necessary to close the diaphragm a bit to cut down the light. Since these cells are transparent, too much light will not give you a clear view. Do you see the dark nucleus in each cell?

Switch to high power and focus on one cell that does not seem to be too much out of shape (Figure 12). Look at the different parts: the nucleus, the cytoplasm, and the cell membrane. You will not see a cell wall; it is found only in plant cells.

BUTTERFLY'S WING • Have you ever touched a butterfly (or a moth) and noticed the dust that collected on your finger? If you can catch one of the common butterflies that visits your neighborhood, you can easily examine this dust under the microscope. (Do not use a rare butterfly; it might become extinct.)

Place a small part of the wing on a slide and add a drop of water and a cover slip. Under low power, you can see numerous scales that overlap like the shingles on a roof. When you touch a butterfly's wing, these scales rub off and appear as dust on your fingers.

For a closer view, gently rub off some of the scales from a wing with the point of a pencil and let them drop onto a slide. Add a drop of water and a cover slip. As you examine the slide, you can see some of the individual scales. Because of the way they overlap, they help the butterfly fly through the air with the least amount of wind resistance.

To make a permanent slide of these scales, scrape some onto a slide and add a drop of Canada balsam and a cover slip. Set the slide aside for two weeks to harden. Attach a label giving the name of the butterfly and the date.

Are all the scales on a butterfly's wing the same size and shape? Compare them under low power. Also compare the scales of this butterfly with those of another type. Are they the same size, shape, and length? Compare them with the scales on a moth's wing.

EYE OF A FLY • A fly has two large eyes called compound eyes because they contain many lenses. To see these lenses, carefully remove the eye of a dead fly with tweezers. Use a sharp razor blade or hobby knife to cut the eye in half.

IN THIS ACTIVITY, BE CAREFUL IN HANDLING THE RAZOR BLADE OR KNIFE AND WORK UNDER

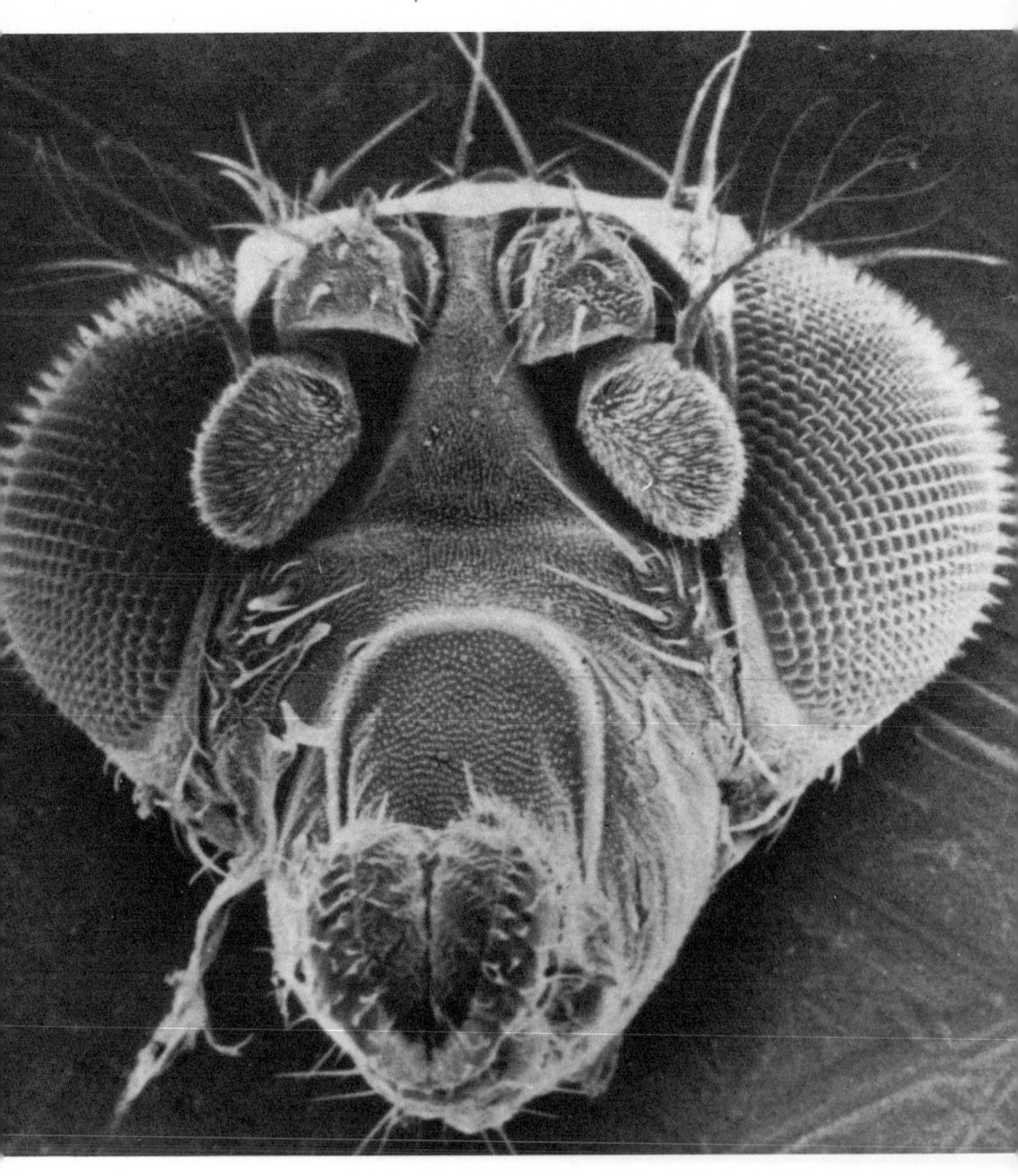

The head of a fruit fly viewed
with an electron microscope

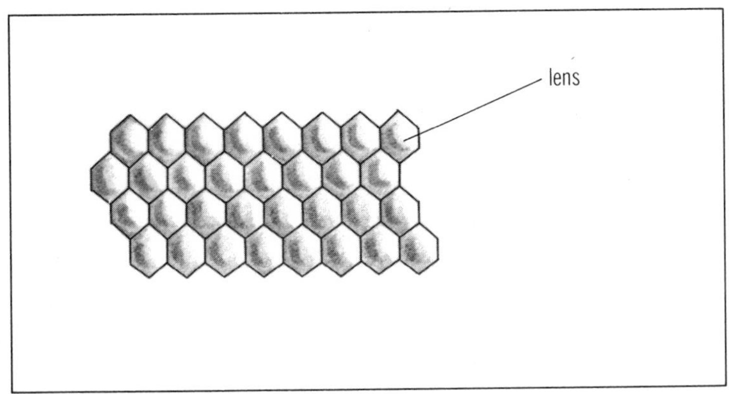

Figure 13. Arrangement of lenses in the compound eye of a fly

ADULT SUPERVISION. IF YOU ARE NOT SURE ABOUT DOING THIS ACTIVITY YOURSELF, ASK A GROWN-UP TO DO IT FOR YOU.

Hold one of the halves with tweezers and dip it in and out of a glass of water to rinse it clean. Place it on a slide; add a drop of water and a cover slip.

Under low power, you can see the neat arrangement of the lenses. How many sides does each lens have? Does the arrangement of lenses remind you of the way the tiles on a bathroom floor appear? Switch to high power and study the shape and structure of a lens (Figure 13).

OTHER PARTS OF A FLY • You will want to see the interesting appearance of the wing, leg, and other parts of a fly under the microscope. Make a permanent slide of these parts, using Canada balsam. Be sure the part is dry. Otherwise, it will become cloudy when Canada balsam is added to it.

BEEF MUSCLE TISSUE • Obtain a small, uncooked piece of beef. Use two needles to spread it apart on a slide as much as you can until you can see small fibers. Add a drop of iodine or ink solution, and a cover slip. Under low power, you can observe the long fibers that make up the beef. Did you know that beef is largely composed of muscle tissue?

Under low power, you should be able to see the cross stripes that make up this type of muscle. These cross stripes consist of alternating dark and light bands. They make the muscle contract and relax whenever it moves. To see the bands more clearly, adjust the diaphragm for just the right amount of light.

Switch to high power for a closeup view. Use the fine adjustment knob to make out some of the nuclei within the muscle fibers (Figure 14).

VOLUNTARY MUSCLES • You have similar muscles in your arms and legs. They are called *voluntary* muscles because they are under your control and you can move them whenever you wish. Other muscles are not under your control, such as those in your heart and in your intestines; they are called *involuntary* muscles.

To learn more about voluntary muscles, take a small piece of meat from an uncooked chicken leg and spread it out on a slide into small fibers with the aid of two needles. Add a drop of iodine or ink so-

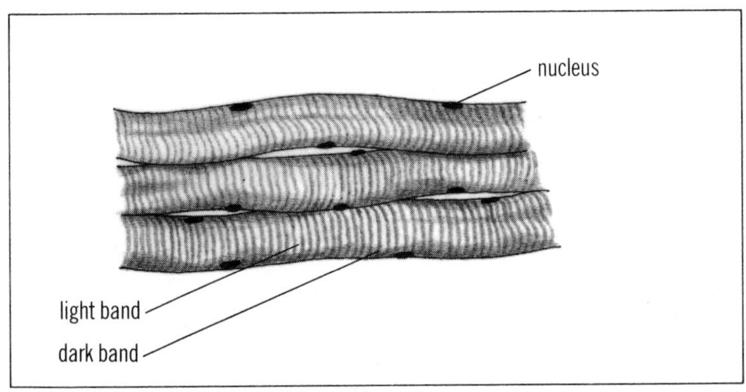

Figure 14. Voluntary muscle fibers showing dark and light bands

lution. Look for the cross stripes under low and high power. Are they similar to those in beef muscle? Examine some of the meat from the breast and the wing. Is it also composed of voluntary or involuntary muscle fibers?

CARTILAGE • Have you ever noticed the smooth, shiny end of the long bone in a chicken leg? This part of the leg is made of *cartilage*. Cartilage plays a useful role in helping the bones move smoothly against each other, without rubbing painfully. We also have cartilage at the ends of the bones in our arms and legs. Cartilage is also found in several other places, including our nose and ear, where it provides support.

HAVE AN ADULT HELP YOU slice a very thin piece of cartilage at the end of a chicken bone. The thinner the slice, the easier it will be to observe the cells with your microscope. Place the slice on a slide, add a drop of ink solution to stain the cells, and cover with a slip.

Under low power, look for cells grouped in twos and threes, which are surrounded by the more solid part of the cartilage. Don't expect to see large masses of cells. Each cell is in its own separate space. Under high power, try to make out the nucleus of the cells. Also observe the structure of the cartilage itself (Figure 15).

Examine thin slices of cartilage from other parts of the chicken such as the breastbone and the bones of the wing. Compare them with a thin slice of cartilage taken from beef bone. Perhaps a butcher can give you some small bones for your scientific study.

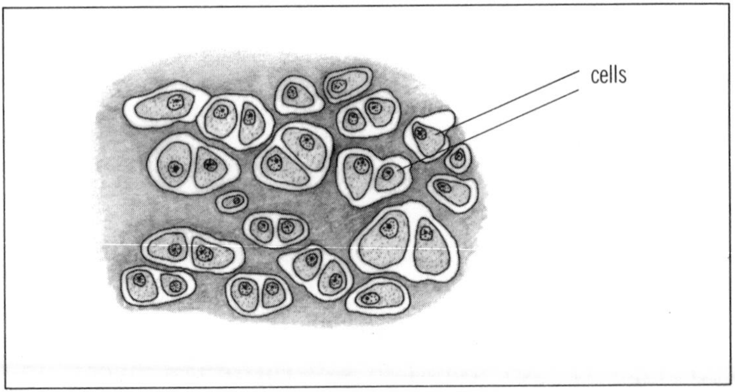

Figure 15. Cartilage. The cells are surrounded by the firm cartilage material.

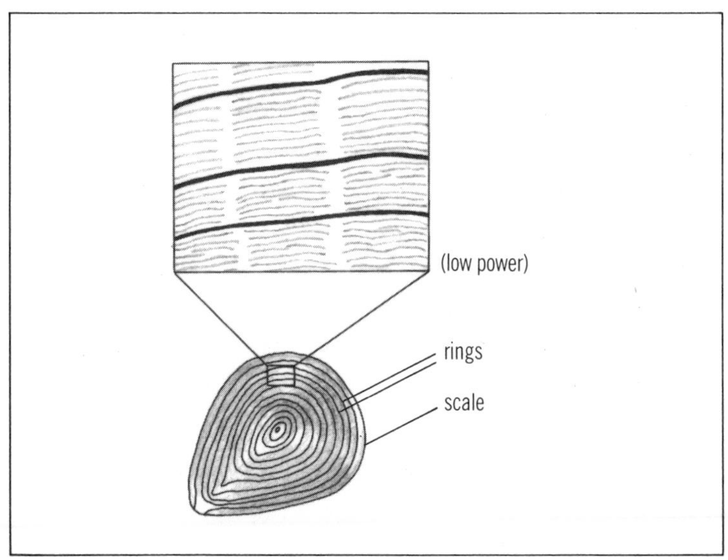

Figure 16. The scale of a fish contains many rings.

FISH SCALES • Fish skin is covered with many scales. If you are unable to catch your own fish, ask the clerk at a fish market or supermarket to remove a few scales from the body of a small fish, such as porgy. Place them in a small envelope and, at home, prepare a slide of one scale in a drop of water. Add a cover slip to flatten it out.

Under low power, observe how the colors of the scale change as you move the mirror back and forth or change the diaphragm opening to let different amounts of light shine on the scales. Do you see rings of lines on the scale (Figure 16)? The older a fish is, the more rings on its scale. As the fish grows, it keeps adding solid material to the scale, increasing the number of the rings. See if you can count the number of rings on the scale.

If a fish has lots of food and is growing rapidly, it will add several rings to each scale in one year. This is different from a tree, which adds only one ring to its width every year.

Try to obtain scales from different types of fish, such as bluefish, cod, or trout. Keep them in different envelopes labeled with their names. Examine the scales under the microscope and compare their rings. Also look for little dark spots which contain pigment, the substance that gives them their color. What is the shape of these pigment cells? Are they all the same size and shape?

BLOOD CIRCULATION • You probably know that the blood circulates in your body because of the pumping action of your heart. How would you like to see blood circulating under the microscope? You can't use your own body, but you can use the tail of a goldfish. The tail is thin and transparent, so that it can easily be studied under the microscope.

You will need to keep the goldfish alive out of the water. Thoroughly wet a piece of absorbent cotton about 3 inches (8 centimeters) square and wrap it around the upper part of the fish's body. The head and gills should be completely covered. This treatment will not hurt the fish if you handle it gently and return it to the water within 10 minutes.

Lay the fish flat on a piece of glass large enough

to cover the stage of the microscope. Or, you may place it in half of a special dish called a petri dish. Cover the tail with a slide to prevent it from flipping about and getting everything wet.

Focus on the tail under low power. Look for blood vessels containing tiny red blood cells moving along quite rapidly. The smallest blood vessels, called *capillaries*, are so narrow that the blood cells move through them in single file. A larger blood vessel may have blood cells moving through in spurts. This is a small *artery*. The blood goes through the arteries in spurts because of the heart's pumping action.

If the blood is moving smoothly through a large blood vessel, you are looking at one of the small *veins*. Look around until you can see the three types of blood vessels. Perhaps you can see small capillaries connected to a small artery or vein.

If you have now kept the fish out of water for 10 minutes, stop your microscopic studies and return the fish to water, where it should swim about actively. If it doesn't, you can help revive the fish by holding its tail and dipping it up and down in the water a few times. This helps bring a fresh flow of water past its gills. You can then continue your observations immediately with another fish.

COFFEE AND THE HEART • As you look at blood spurting through a small artery, count the number of times it spurts in 1 minute. This tells you what its "pulse" is or how many times the heart beats in 1 minute. See if you can speed up the pulse beat with coffee. The caffeine in coffee stimulates the heartbeat in people.

Will it have the same effect on the fish? Add 10 drops of coffee to the wet absorbent cotton covering the head of the fish. The coffee will be absorbed into the blood of the fish through the gills. Wait about 2 minutes and then count the beats.

A DROP OF BLOOD • A drop of blood contains such a tremendous amount of red blood cells that there is a special way of preparing a slide. First obtain a small piece of fresh beef liver from a butcher or supermarket. Let a drop of blood from it drop onto one end of a clean slide. Touch the end of another slide to the drop and use it to draw the blood along the length of the slide. It should spread out in a broad, very thin layer of blood (Figure 17). This smear should have a light yellowish color; if it appears reddish, it is probably too thick. You may have to practice the technique a bit before it comes out just right.

After the blood smear has dried, examine it under low power. You can now see countless numbers of tiny red blood cells. They are round and light pink in color. Add a drop of blue-ink solution to the slide and cover with a slip. The center of a red blood cell appears lighter in color because this is the thinnest part of the cell. There is no nucleus in these red blood cells.

However, if you can locate some white blood cells, you should be able to see a nucleus in them. These cells are larger than red blood cells, but not as numerous. If you move the slide, you may be able to see several types of white blood cells with nuclei of different shapes.

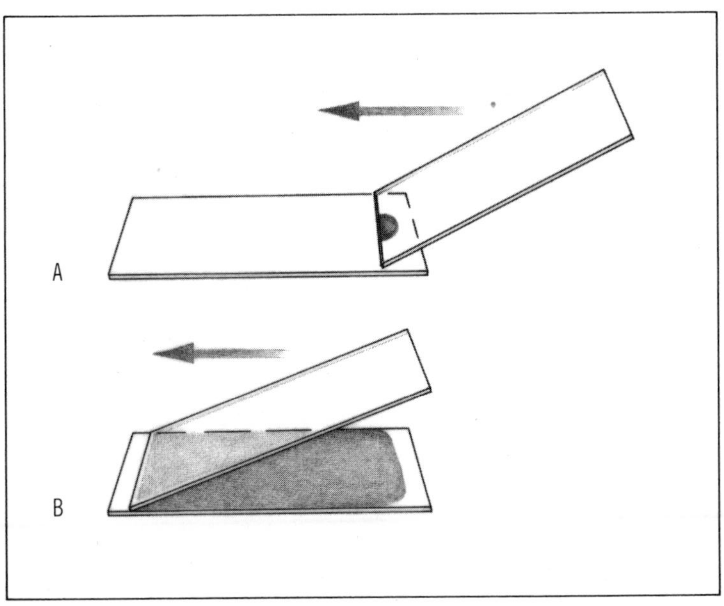

Figure 17. Preparation of a blood smear

A more detailed study of blood can be made with Wright's stain, a professional stain. It stains the cytoplasm of one type of white blood cell red, another type blue, and the nucleus of most white blood cells a deep blue.

COMPARING BLOOD CELLS • Compare drops of blood from different specimens, for example, fish, poultry, or meat other than beef. Make a blood smear on a slide the same way you did before. Under low power, what is the shape of their red blood cells? Are they the same size? View under high power. Do you see a nucleus in them?

DO THE FOLLOWING ONLY UNDER ADULT SUPERVISION AND AFTER OBTAINING THE PERMISSION OF ONE OF YOUR PARENTS. Perhaps you would like to look at a drop of your own blood. Rub the end of your little finger with a small piece of absorbent cotton soaked in rubbing alcohol. Have the adult sterilize a needle by heating the tip for a moment in a gas flame or a match flame. Now there are no germs on either the needle tip or the skin of your finger.

Quickly jab the needle into the soft part of the side of the fingertip. This should be practically painless. Squeeze the finger until there is a bright-red drop of blood. Deposit the drop at one end of a clean slide and make a thin smear of it. To prevent germs from getting into the pinprick, wipe the end of the finger with a little tincture of iodine.

Examine the blood smear under low and high power. How does human blood compare with the blood from cattle (from which beef liver is obtained)? Do the red blood cells have the same size and shape?

DISCARD THE COTTON, NEEDLE, AND SLIDE WHEN YOU ARE THROUGH. DO NOT USE THE SAME NEEDLE TO TAKE BLOOD FROM ANYONE ELSE.

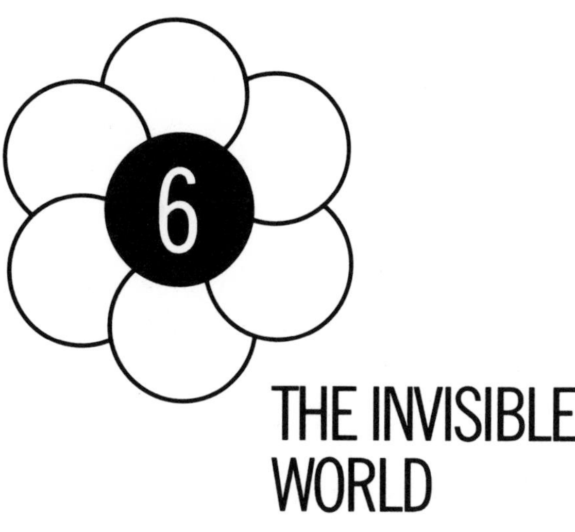

THE INVISIBLE WORLD

LIFE IN A DROP OF POND WATER • It may be hard to believe, but a drop of water from a pond is swarming with tiny living things that move about actively here and there. It is a fascinating, normally invisible world filled with different types of one-celled creatures called *protozoa*. Although composed of only one cell, they have special parts that enable them to move about, take in and digest food, excrete wastes, and reproduce. Also in pond water are tiny green plantlike cells called *algae*, which may grow either as long threads or as individual cells.

To begin your study of these microscopic living things, collect water in a wide-mouthed jar or plastic container from the edge of a pond, stream, river, or brook where the water is shallow and contains green material growing in it. Also scoop up a little of the dirt near the bottom of the water.

Keep the jar on a window sill or a table where there is light, but *not* in the direct rays of the sun. Direct sunlight might cook your specimen. From the top of the jar, place a drop of water containing some of the green material on a slide; add a cover slip. Look at it under low power. Do you see a new world here? Some of the protozoa dart about rapidly. Others move more slowly. Some appear to be stationary. The green material is now seen as slender filaments of algae. Occasionally you may find a thin worm thrashing about.

Scientists have given names to the various types of microscopic living things. You may want to learn to recognize them (see Figure 18):

paramecium—a slipper-shaped protozoan that moves about quickly.

spirostomum—a very long, narrow protozoan that seems to glide along and then reverse its direction.

vorticella—a bell-like protozoan whose fine stalk is usually attached to some algae or plant surface. The stalk contracts suddenly when it is disturbed.

amoeba—a simple gray protozoan that does not have a particular shape, but keeps changing its form as it moves along very slowly.

spirogyra—a green filament of algae named for its spiral-shaped chloroplasts.

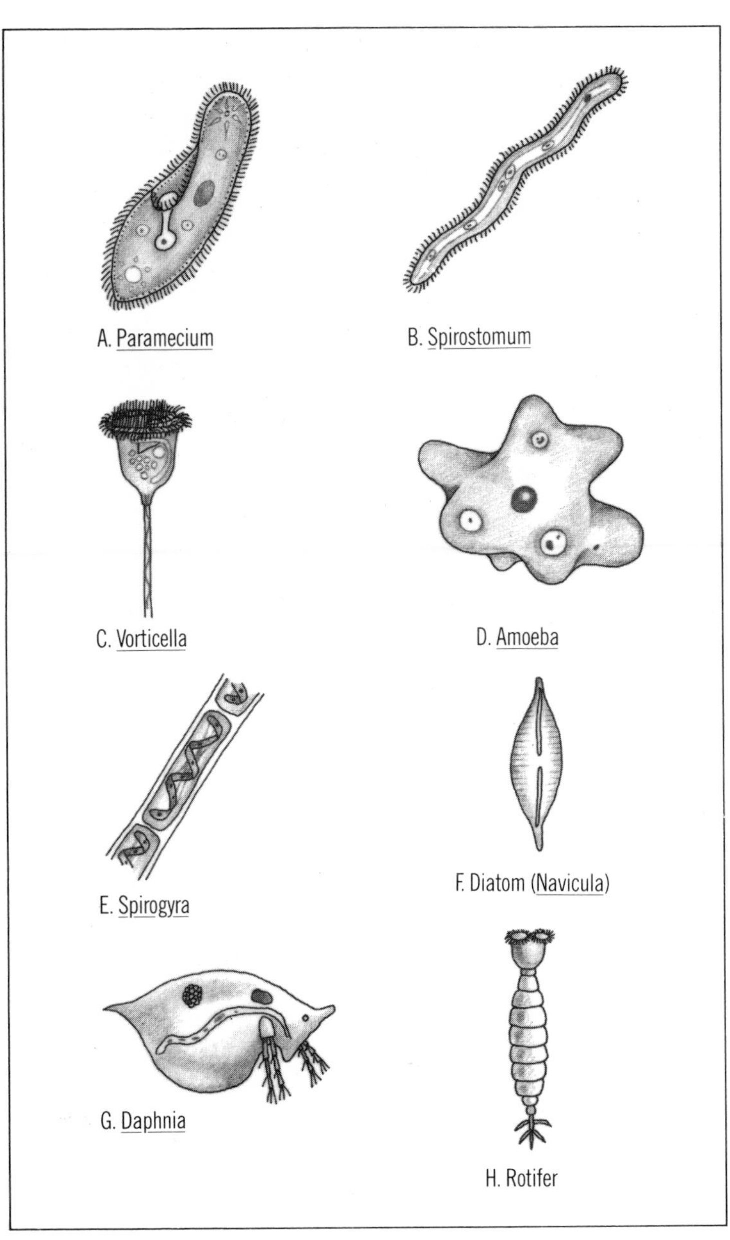

Figure 18. Some of the living things in a drop of pond water

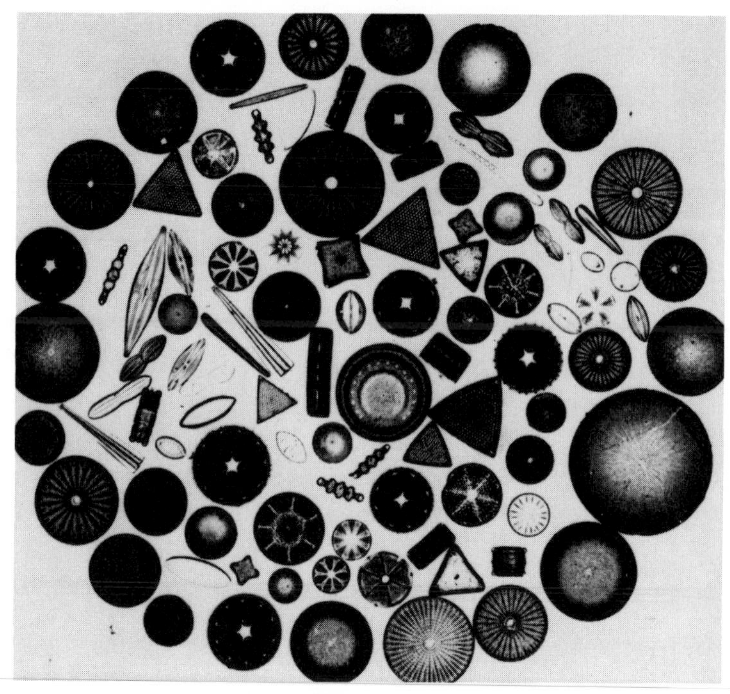

Diatoms **(magnified)**

diatom—a single-celled alga that sometimes has attractive designs with parallel markings.

daphnia—also called water flea; you can see it with your naked eye since it's about the size of the head of a pin; it darts through the water with jerky movements.

rotifer—a tiny, many-celled animal that has rotating, wheellike structures at one end and that moves by contracting itself.

You may not see all of these in the same water sample, but you probably will see other types of living things as well, as you keep observing different drops of water.

Now examine a drop of pond water that includes a little of the top layer of dirt found at the bottom of the jar. You will probably see different organisms, along with those you have seen before. Keep moving the slide to discover additional specimens. Also try water samples from different locations, at different times of the year.

PARAMECIA • Let's turn our attention to *Paramecium*, one of the best-known protozoa. You can easily grow your own culture in this way: To start, obtain a small amount of paramecium culture (*Paramecium* is the scientific name, paramecium and paramecia—the plural of paramecium—the common names) from a science teacher or from one of the companies listed at the back of the book. Then allow half a jar of tap water to stand exposed to the air overnight; this is to get rid of any chlorine it may contain. (Chlorine is added to drinking water to kill any germs in it.)

Now squirt a small amount of the paramecium culture into the jar of water with a medicine dropper. Break a brewer's yeast tablet (which you can obtain in a drugstore or supermarket) in half and crumble one of the halves into the water. This will serve as food for the paramecia. As they feed on it, they will grow and reproduce by simply dividing in half. Set the jar away from direct sunlight and in 7 to 10 days the water in the jar will be cloudy with thousands of

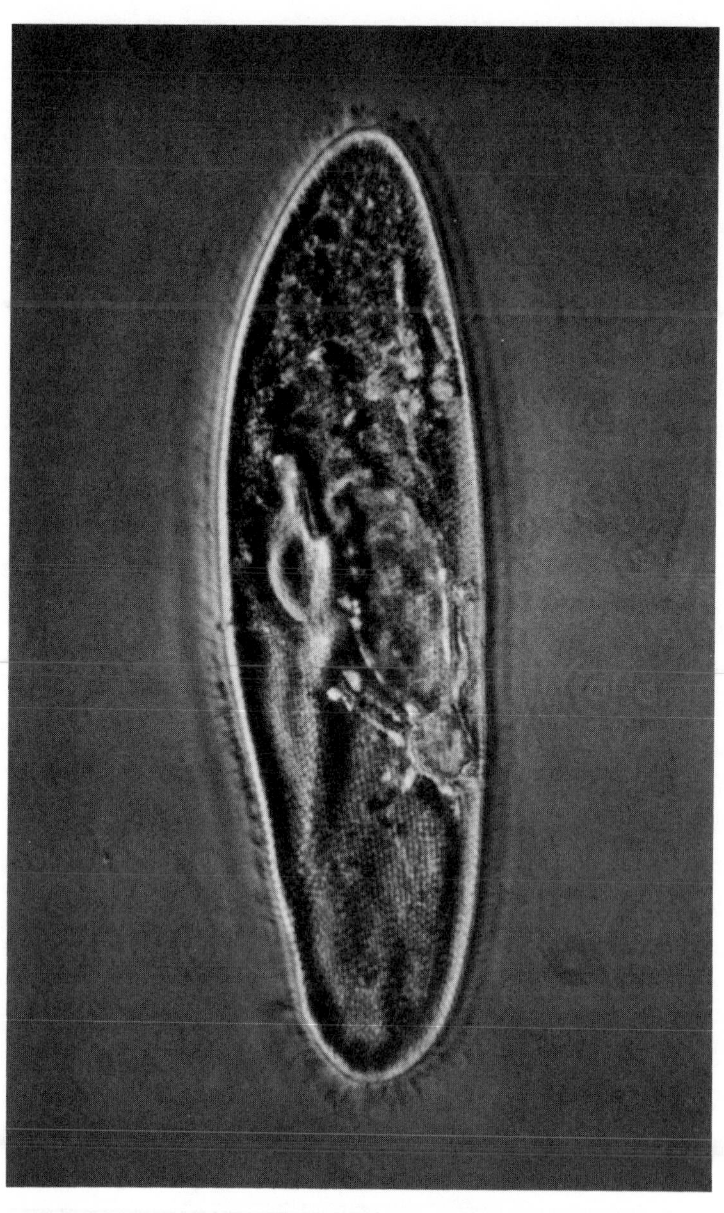

A *Paramecium* (magnified)

tiny specks of paramecia. You now have a paramecium culture.

Place a drop of the culture on a slide. Slip a piece of black construction paper under the slide. With your naked eye, can you see the little white specks moving about against this black background? Remove the black paper and add a cover slip to the drop. Examine under low power. Magnified 100 times, the tiny specks have now become large paramecia. Each speeds by in different directions. They go so fast that it is hard to study them. Move the slide to try to keep up with them.

Occasionally, you may find one moving slowly. If you cut down on the light with the diaphragm, you may be able to see the *cilia*, the little hairlike structures that enable the paramecium to move. These cilia cover its surface and beat rapidly, like tiny oars, pushing it through the water.

There is a simple way to slow paramecia down. Take a small piece of lens paper about the size of a cover slip and, holding its ends firmly, pull it apart carefully in the middle until it almost separates in half. It is now held together by small shreds of the paper. Put it on a slide and add a drop of the paramecium culture to the middle part which was torn apart. Add a cover slip and focus under low power.

Now you can see the paramecia being slowed down by the fibers of the paper. They keep bumping into the paper threads which block their path. As they meet a paper fiber, they reverse direction and travel in the opposite way. They stop more often, making it easier for you to study them.

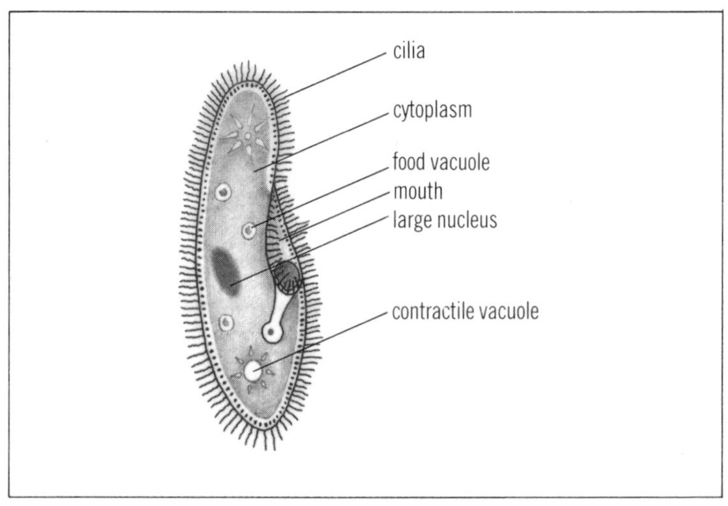

Figure 19. ***Paramecium.*** **Although it consists of only one cell, it has many parts.**

Here is your chance to really examine their structure (Figure 19). Do you see the cilia beating rapidly? Near the middle of the paramecium, you may see its "mouth," a wide funnel lined with cilia. As they beat inward, they create a current in the water that sweeps up little food particles into a special part called a *food vacuole*. When this structure fills up with food, it is taken in and moved around within the cytoplasm. The food is digested in the cytoplasm to help the paramecium grow and move about. How many food vacuoles can you count?

If you find a paramecium that has stopped gliding about, move the slide until it is in the center of the field and switch to high power. Look for the rapidly beating cilia along the sides and in the mouth. Can you see a food vacuole filling up with food particles at the end of the mouth?

By now, you have probably noticed a little, clear round structure near one end of the organism. As you watch it, it appears to grow and suddenly contract. Soon afterward, it repeats the process, growing and contracting. Because of this activity, it is called the *contractile vacuole*. Its job is to get rid of excess water that the paramecium keeps taking in. You may be able to make out little canals surrounding it. Look for another contractile vacuole at the other end of the organism.

OTHER PROTOZOA • Make a similar study of other protozoa that you find in your water sample. Perhaps you can obtain a pure culture of some of them from a science teacher or a scientific supply company. Do they all move by cilia?

Can you identify food vacuoles and contractile vacuoles? Perhaps you will be able to observe some protozoa dividing in half, as they reproduce.

SPIROGYRA • If your water sample contains some fine, green silky threads, chances are that you have an alga called *Spirogyra*.

Prepare a slide of *Spirogyra*. Add a drop of water and a cover slip. Under low power, find one of the long filaments. Notice the bright-green color of the spiral-shaped chloroplast, which winds around within a cell. Sometimes, there are two such spiral chloro-

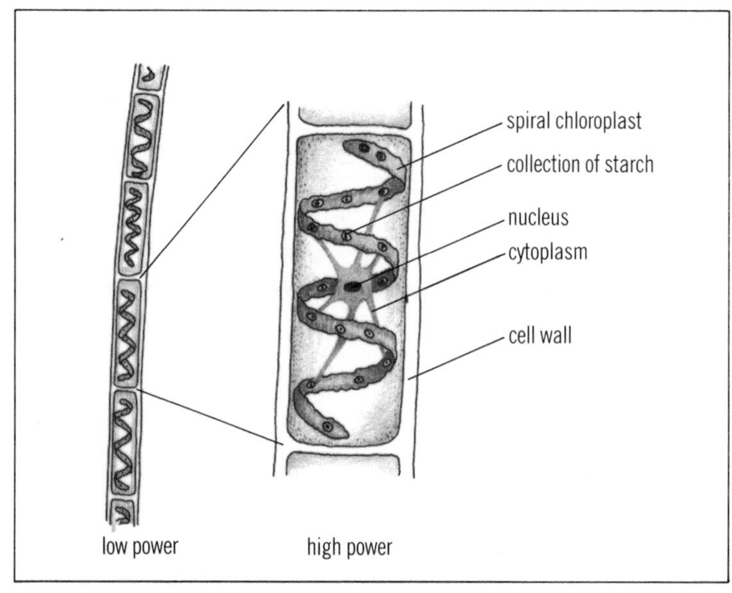

Figure 20. *Spirogyra* grow in long filaments and have spiral, ribbon-like chloroplasts in each cell.

plasts, winding in opposite directions. Do you see many cells lined up to form the length of the thread-like filament?

Switch to high power and study the structure of one of the cells. Keep turning the fine adjustment knob, and open or close the diaphragm for the best light. Can you make out other parts of the cell, such as the nucleus, cytoplasm, cell wall, and dotlike structures along the chloroplast (Figure 20)?

Add a drop of iodine solution with a medicine

dropper to the *side* of the cover slip (not on top of it) so that the solution spreads under it. After a minute, view the spirogyra under low power to see if the chloroplast shows up more clearly. If it does, it is because its job is to manufacture starch. As you may remember, iodine turns starch a deep blue-black color.

Under high power, you may be able to see dark blue-black little dots along the length of the chloroplasts, showing where the starch collected. Also look for the nucleus, usually in the center of the cell. Can you see it surrounded by the cytoplasm? Also, can you see thin strands of cytoplasm spreading out from it to the other parts of the cell?

OTHER ALGAE • Since algae contain chlorophyll (the green coloring matter in the chloroplasts), you may use this color to locate other algae in your water sample. Some may appear as slim green filaments, like *Spirogyra*, but without a spiral-shaped chloroplast. Others will appear as small, single cells.

Among the more attractive are the diatoms. These small algae have cell walls made of silica, a substance found in sand. If you are patient, you may find several types of them in your sample. You can recognize them by their beautiful markings and shapes, making them look like tiny jewels. Diatoms, like other algae, are especially important because of their ability to make their own food; therefore, living things unable to do this eat them and depend on them for their existence.

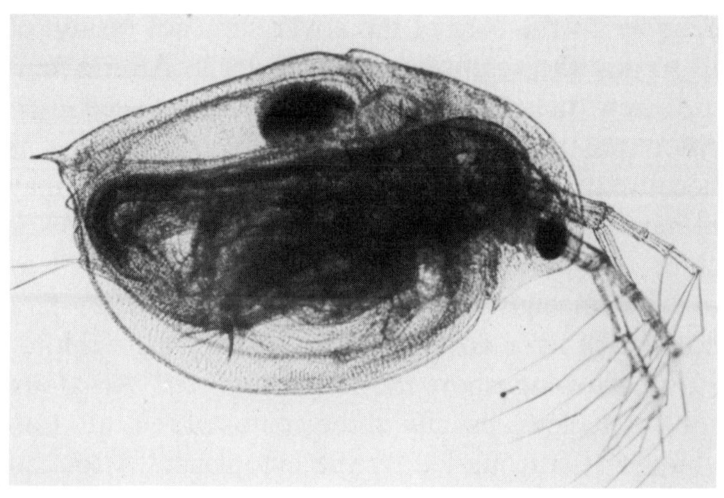

***Daphnia*, a water flea (*magnified*)**

DAPHNIA • Among the interesting living things in pond water is the water flea, *Daphnia*. This tiny animal, about the size of a pinhead, can be seen darting through the water in a jerky motion. A daphnia is much larger than the paramecium and is actually a many-celled animal. It is a miniature relative of such animals as the crab and the lobster. If you do not see it in your sample of water, you may be able to buy some in a pet shop, where they are sold as live food for tropical fish, or from a scientific supply company.

First look at a daphnia in the water with your naked eye and watch it flitting about. Then quickly scoop it up into the end of a medicine dropper. Transfer it to a slide in a drop of water. However, *do not add a cover slip*—it would flatten the daphnia out and kill it. Since it cannot move very much in the small drop of water, you will be able to observe it without the use of a cover slip.

View it under low power (Figure 21). Notice the two long leglike antennae. They propel the daphnia through the water in its rapid, jerky movements. *Daphnia* has a transparent, brownish shell, so you can see its insides quite clearly. Trace the length of its digestive canal. Look for the small mass of eggs above it. How many eggs can you count? Look for the eye; it is composed of many tiny lenses.

The heart, located in the back, keeps beating rapidly. Can you count the number of times it beats in 1 minute? After 5 minutes, count the heartbeat again and see if it has changed, because of the animal's captivity on the slide.

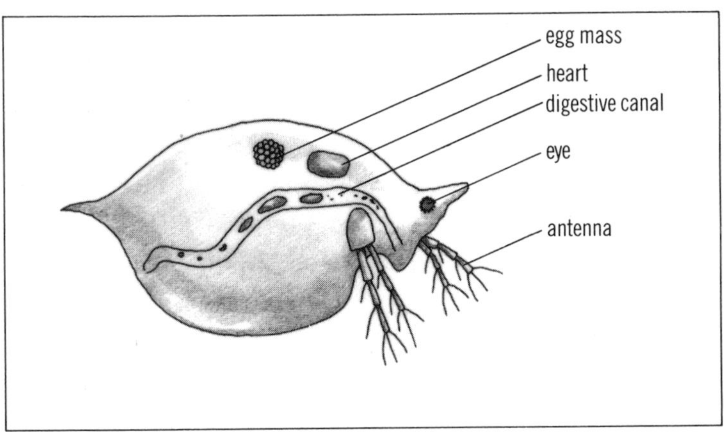

Figure 21. *Daphnia*, a water flea, is a many-celled animal with different organs.

See if you can change the heartbeat of a daphnia. Use a medicine dropper to add a drop of ordinary (nondecaffeinated) coffee to the drop of water on the slide. After a minute, count the heartbeat again. How has the coffee affected the heartbeat? Now prepare a slide with another daphnia. Make a record of its heartbeat rate. Add a drop of decaffeinated coffee. Wait a minute and count the heartbeat again. Since there is very little caffeine in this coffee, does it affect the heartbeat as much as ordinary coffee? Compare the results with substances such as aspirin, sugar, and tea.

YEAST • Yeast is used in baking bread and cake because it gives off carbon dioxide gas. This gas makes the dough rise and become fluffy. Otherwise, it would remain solid and flat. You can obtain yeast as either a small cake or powder from a grocery store. Add a pinch of it to half a glass of water containing a teaspoon of sugar. Let the water stand overnight in a warm place. The yeast cells feed on the sugar, grow, and multiply.

To examine yeast cells under the microscope, place a small drop of the yeast liquid on a slide. Add a drop of water to spread the numerous cells apart and cover with a slip. Under low power, you will see countless tiny yeast cells. Look for an area of the slide where they are not too crowded, and switch to high power. Now you can pick out several for close study (Figure 22).

Look for a cell that has another little cell, called a bud, attached to it. The bud will grow until it is the

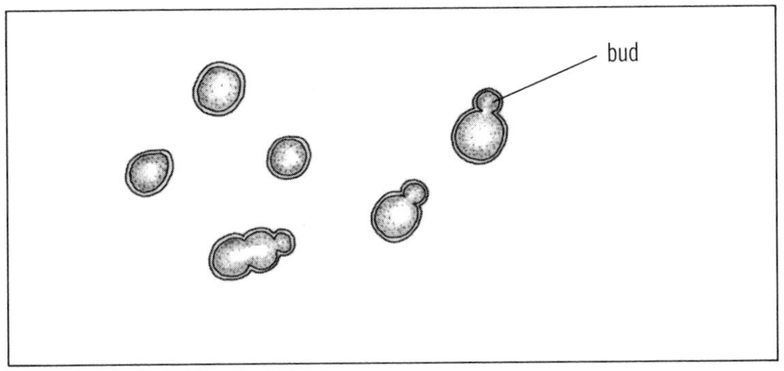

Figure 22. Yeast cells are very small and reproduce by forming buds.

same size as the original cell and then it will also form a bud. Do you see several buds attached to one yeast cell? Yeast reproduces by budding.

Look inside the yeast cell. You may have to adjust the diaphragm to get the best light. Try adding a drop of iodine solution to the slide and see if the parts are more visible. Keep using the fine adjustment knob. The large clear area is called a *vacuole*. It is used by the cell to store food.

Yeast cells are small compared with paramecia. Add a drop from a culture of each to a slide, cover with a slip, and you can make some interesting observations. First, you will be able to compare the size of each. Then if you have a great many yeast cells on the slide, the paramecia have to force their way past them as they move around. Cut down on the light a bit by adjusting the diaphragm, and you should be able to see the cilia helping the paramecia push through the crowd of yeast cells. Estimate how many yeast cells placed side by side would equal the length of one paramecium.

BREAD MOLD • You can grow your own bread mold if you start with a small jar that has a tight-fitting cover. Line the bottom of the jar with moist newspaper. Place half a slice of fresh bread or roll into the jar so that it leans against the side. Use bread or rolls that have no preservatives to keep them from spoiling.

Sprinkle some dust on the bread. Close the cover tightly so that the newspaper does not dry out. Leave the jar at room temperature, away from direct sunlight. Look at it every day. After a week or so, you will find the bread becoming covered with some white, fluffy material that looks like cobwebs. This is the bread mold that is starting to grow. When little black dots appear throughout the growth, you are ready to examine the bread mold with your microscope.

Open the jar and use tweezers to remove only a small amount of the mold from the sides of the jar. Place it on a drop of water on a slide. Try not to crush the material. Add a cover slip and examine under low power (Figure 23).

Do you see a tangle of threadlike structures? Focus on one thread and trace it to its end, where there should be a large, ball-like structure, the *spore case*. The case will be filled with countless tiny cells called spores. If you broke the spore case when you

Bread mold (*magnified*). The black round objects are spore cases.

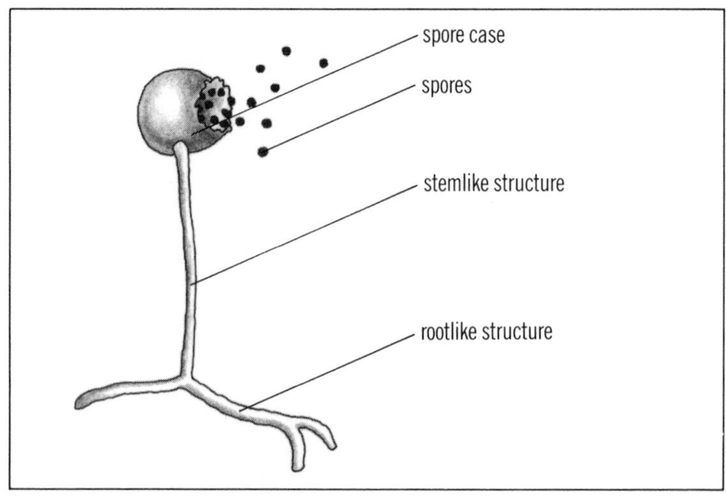

Figure 23. Bread mold forms countless spores.

prepared the slide, you will probably see numerous spores all over the slide. At the opposite end of one of the threads you should be able to see a rootlike structure. This is attached to the bread, which provides the food for the mold.

The spores are so tiny that you cannot see them without a microscope. They float in the air on dust particles. That is why you were able to start the mold growing when you added dust to the bread. Switch to high power and examine a spore. It has a thick wall that keeps its cytoplasm from drying up. When the spore lands in a moist spot with food, it starts to develop into a new bread mold.

OTHER MOLDS • Another mold that is easy to grow is the blue-green mold, *Penicillium*. Line the bottom of a small jar with a layer of moist newspaper. Add a piece of fruit (a quarter of an orange or an apple), and sprinkle it with some dust. Cover the jar tightly. After a week or so, examine the mold that has developed. Under low power, look for the spore case. How is it different from the spore case of bread mold? This mold has become famous because it supplies us with the important drug penicillin, which protects us from disease germs. It is also the mold that gives blue-green Roquefort cheese its particular flavor. Do you see any other molds? What color are they? Study them with your microscope.

BACTERIA • Bacteria are so tiny that it takes lots of practice with the microscope for you to be able to see them. But by this time, after viewing so many different microscopic organisms, you are undoubtedly ready to take on the smallest of all cells. These are the bacteria, which come in three types: rod-shaped; ball-shaped; and spiral-shaped (Figure 24).

BACTERIA ON YOUR TEETH ○ Let's start with the bacteria attached to the teeth in your own mouth. Use the blunt end of a toothpick to *gently* scrape off some of the white stuff that clings to the teeth in the back of your mouth, at the gum line. Spread this material across the middle of a slide, add a drop of your saliva, and cover with a slip. Under low power, locate the collections of material scattered through the slide.

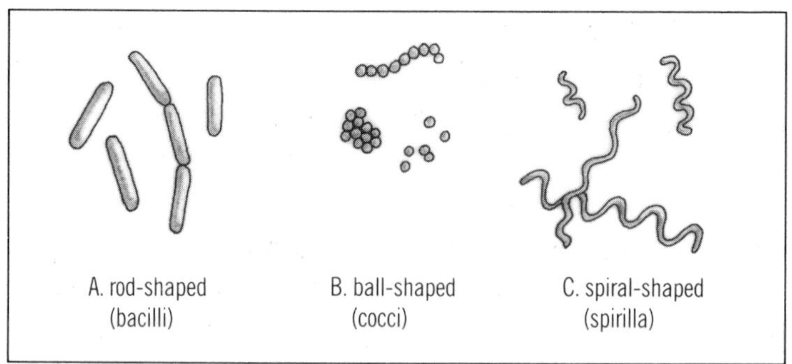

Figure 24. Three types of bacteria

You may recognize cells with an irregular shape. Do these remind you of cheek cells? These particular cells are from the surface of the gums. Cut down on the light with the diaphragm so that the small details become clearer. Search for areas between the larger cheek cells until your eye makes out the colorless, tiny, rod-shaped bacteria. Such rod-shaped bacteria are called *bacilli*.

Switch to high power and regulate the diaphragm again for the best view. Keep adjusting the fine adjustment knob as you focus on the bacilli. You may see them moving, wriggling, and turning about.

If you think it is difficult to see bacteria, remember that Leeuwenhoek was the first person to see them, three hundred years ago, by scraping them from his own teeth. And his was a simple microscope, with only one lens and less powerful than your compound microscope.

Prepare another slide, and this time add a drop of blue ink solution to stain the bacteria. Do they now seem clearer under high power?

BACTERIA IN HAY WATER ○ You can start a culture of bacteria growing in this way: Allow half a jar of water to remain uncovered overnight to get rid of any chlorine. Place some hay or dried grass in the water. After about five days, you will notice that the water has turned cloudy and has a thin film on the surface.

Remove some of this film with a medicine dropper and examine it under low and high power. Do you see long bacilli? Are they separate or connected to one another to make a chain? Can you see them moving or wriggling about?

BACTERIA IN YOGURT ○ Yogurt is prepared from milk by treating it with a certain strain of bacteria. Obtain a small container of low-fat yogurt at the dairy section of the grocery or supermarket. Place a small drop on a slide. Now add a drop of water to dilute it. Cover with a slip and examine with low power. Look between the masses of yogurt for tiny, rod-shaped bacteria.

Switch to high power. Use the fine adjustment knob constantly as you study these bacilli. You may have to adjust the diaphragm for the best light. While you are looking at the bacteria, some of them may seem to disappear as they move down into the liquid. Try to follow their movement by slowly turning the fine adjustment knob downward. Other bacteria may appear to move slowly or wriggle about.

BACTERIA IN OTHER FOODS ○ Buttermilk is also made by the action of bacteria on milk. Mix a small drop of buttermilk with two drops of water on a slide and cover with a slip. Under high power, compare the size, shape, and arrangement of the bacteria with the size, shape, and arrangement of the bacteria you saw in yogurt. Similarly, sauerkraut is made from strips of cabbage that have been treated with bacteria. Examine a drop of juice from fresh sauerkraut (not canned). Study the size, shape, and movement of the bacteria.

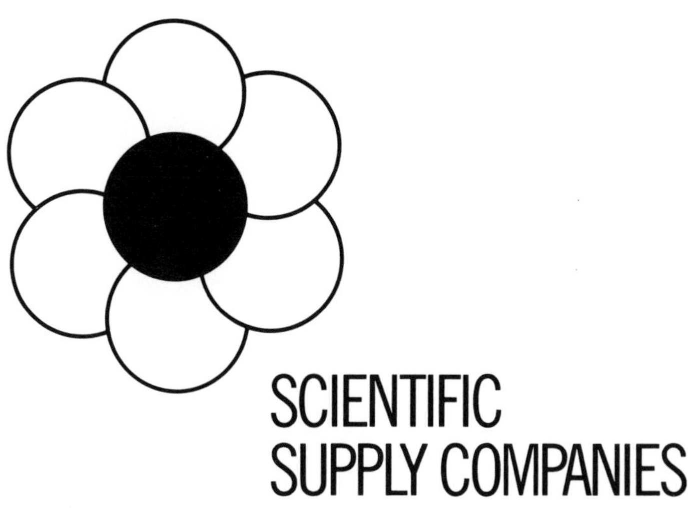

SCIENTIFIC SUPPLY COMPANIES

The following companies sell microscopes, supplies such as slides and stains, and living protozoa, algae, microscopic animals, and other specimens.

If you wish to order any materials from these companies, first write to the Customer Service Department of the company nearest your home and inquire about prices. Then, after you have received a reply, send them a check or money order for the required amount, along with your order. Another way is to ask your teacher to write to the company on school letterhead.

Some companies will send free catalogues; others charge several dollars. Either way, it is well worth your while to obtain your own catalogue.

Carolina Biological Supply Company, 2700 York Ave., Burlington, NC 27215; also: Powell Laboratories Division of Carolina Biological Supply Company, Gladstone, OR 97027

College Biological Supply Co., 8857 Mount Israel Rd., Escondido, CA 92025

Connecticut Valley Biological Supply Co., 82 Valley Rd., P.O. Box 326, Southampton, MA 01073

Delta Biologicals, P.O. Box 26666, Tuscon, AZ 85726–6666

Delta Education, P.O. Box M, Nashua, NH 03061–6012

Edmund Scientific, 4145 Edscorp Bldg., Barrington, NJ 08007

Fisher Scientific Co., Educational Materials Division, 4901 W. LeMoyne St., Chicago, IL 60651

Frey Scientific Co., 905 Hickory Ln., Mansfield, OH 44905

Grau-Hall Scientific Corp., 6501 Elvas Ave., Sacramento, CA 95819

Learning Alternatives, P.O. Box 219, Vienna, OH 44473

McKilligan Supply Corp., 435 Main St., Johnson City, NY 13790

NASCO, 901 Janesville Ave., Fort Atkinson, WI 53538

Nasco West, P.O. Box 3837, Modesto, CA 95352

Sargent-Welch Scientific Co., 7300 N. Linder Ave., Skokie, IL 60077

Schoolmasters Science, 745 State Circle, P.O. Box 1941, Ann Arbor, MI 48106

Science Kit and Boreal Labs, 777 E. Park Dr., Tonawanda, NY 14150

Southern Biological Supply Co., McKenzie, TN 38201

Ward's Natural Science Establishment, 5100 West Henrietta Rd., P. O. Box 92912, Rochester, NY 14692–9012; also: 11850 East Florence Ave., Santa Fe Springs (LA), CA 90670–4490

FOR FURTHER READING

Anderson, Margaret Dampier. *Through the Microscope.* Garden City, N.Y.: Natural History Press, 1965.

Beeler, Nelson F., and Branley, Franklyn M. *Experiments with a Microscope.* New York: Thomas Y. Crowell, 1957.

Bradbury, Savile. *The Microscope: Past and Present.* New York: Pergamon Press, 1968.

Corrington, Julian D. *Exploring with Your Microscope.* New York: McGraw-Hill, 1957.

Cowhig, Jerry. *The World under the Microscope.* New York: Bounty Books, 1974.

Curry, Alan. *Under the Microscope*. New York: Van Nostrand Reinhold, 1982.

DeKruif, Paul. *Microbe Hunters*. New York: Harcourt Brace, 1966.

Delly, John G. *Photography through the Microscope*. Rochester, N.Y.: Eastman Kodak, 1980.

Dobell, Clifford. *Antony van Leeuwenhoek and His "Little Animals."* New York: Dover, 1932.

Goldstein, Philip, and Metzner, Jerome. *Experiments with Microscopic Animals*. New York: Doubleday, 1971.

Gravé, Eric V. *Discover the Invisible: A Naturalist's Guide to Using the Microscope*. Englewood Cliffs, N.J.: Prentice-Hall, 1984.

Gray, Peter. *The Encyclopedia of Microscopy and Microtechnique*. New York: Krieger, 1973.

Grillone, Lisa. *Small Worlds Close Up*. New York: Crown, 1978.

Harrison, C. William. *The Microscope*. New York: Messner, 1965.

Hartley, Walter G. *How to Use a Microscope*. Garden City, N.Y.: Natural History Press, 1964.

Headstrom, Richard. *Adventures with a Microscope*. New York: Dover, 1977.

Jirovec, D.; Boucek, B.; and Fiala, F. *Life under the Microscope*. London: Spring Books, 1969.

Johnson, Gaylord; Bleifeld, Maurice; and Beller, Joel. *Hunting with the Microscope*. 3rd ed. New York: Arco, 1980.

Kudo, Richard R. *Protozoology*, 5th ed. Springfield, Ill.: Charles C. Thomas, 1977.

Needham, George H. *The Practical Use of the Microscope*. Springfield, Ill.: Charles C. Thomas, 1977.

Needham, James G., and Needham, Paul R. *Guide to the Study of Fresh Water Biology*, 5th ed. San Francisco: Holden-Day, 1962.

Patent, Dorothy H. *Microscopic Animals and Plants*. New York: Holiday House, 1974.

Pinney, Roy. *Collecting and Photographing Your Microzoo*. Cleveland: World, 1965.

Stehli, George. *The Microscope and How to Use It*. New York: Dover, 1970.

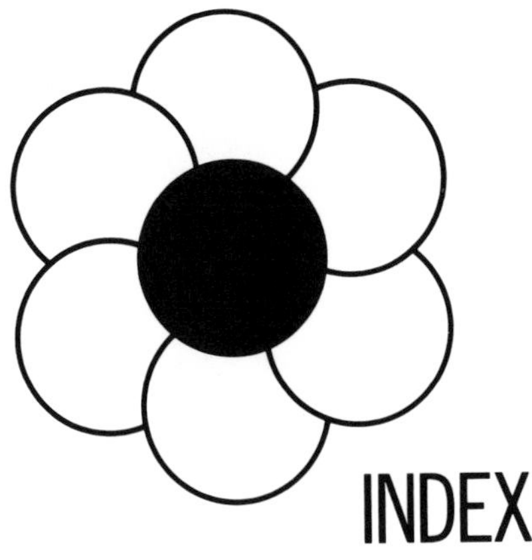

INDEX

Pages numbers in italics indicate illustrations.

Algae, 20, 77, 85–87
Amoeba, 78
Animals, looking at, 63–76. *See also specific animals*
Anthrax, 22
Arm, 26
Arteries, 73

Bacilli, 96
Bacteria, 95–98; as cause of disease, 20, 22; discovery of, 16, 20
Base, 26
Beef muscle tissue, 68
Blood cells, 72–76
Body tube, 27

Bread mold, 92, *93*, *94*
Butterfly's wing, 64–65

Canada balsam, 30–31
Capillaries, 73
Cartilage, 69, *70*
Cell(s): animal, 63–76; discovery of, 16, 19–20; plant, 49–61
Cell membrane, 52
Cell theory, 20
Cell wall, 51
Cheek cells, 63–*64*
Chlorophyll, 87
Chloroplasts, 52–54, 85–*86*, 87
Cilia, 83, 85
Coffee, heartbeat stimulated by, 73–74
Compound microscopes, 19, 25–37; making slides, 28–32; parts of, *26*–28; using the, 32–37
Contractile vacuole, 85
Cork cells, 19, 49–50
Corn starch grains, 55–56
Cotton fibers, 41
Course adjustment knob, 28, 34
Cover slip, 28, *29*, *30*, 37
Crystals, 39–40
Cytoplasm, 52, 53, 75, 84

Dandelion seed and its parachute hair, 60–*61*
Daphnia, 80, *88*, *89*, 90
Diaphragm, 28, 35, 36
Diatoms, *80*, 87
Disease, bacteria as cause of, 20, 22
Do's and don'ts in using the microscope, 36–37
Drop of blood, 74–*75*

Electron microscopes, *23*–*24*
Elodea leaf, 52, *53*, 54
England, 16, 19
Eyeglasses, 36
Eye of a fly, 65, *66*, *67*
Eyepiece, 26, 34
Eye strain, 36

Fibers, textile, 41–45
Fine adjustment knob, 28, 35, 36
Fish scales, *71*–72
Fly, 65, *66*, *67*, 68

Foods, bacteria in, 97–98
Food vacuole, 84, 85
France, 20
Fruit skins, 59–60

Germany, 19, 20
Green plant cells, 52, *53*, 54

Hair, 40–41, *42*
Hay water, bacteria in, 97
Heartbeat, coffee stimulation of, 73–74
High-power objective, 27, 32, 35–36, 37
History of microscopes, 13–24
Holland, 13, 15, 16
Hooke, Richard, 16–19, 24, 49; microscope and drawings of, *17*, *18*, 19

Immunization, 22
Involuntary muscles, 68

Leeuwenhoek, Anton van, 13, *14*, 15–16, 19, 20, 24, 96; microscopes of, *15*, 16
Low-power objective, 27, 32, 34, 35, 37

Magnification, 27, 34–36, 37
Making slides, 28–32
Micrographia (Hooke), 19
Mirror, 27–28
Molds, 92–95

Nosepiece, 27
Nucleus, 51, 75

Objectives, 27
Oil immersion objective, 27
Onion cells, 50, *51*, 52

Paramecium, 78, 81, *82*, 83, *84*, 85, 91, 92
Parts of the microscope, *26*–28
Pasteur, Louis, 20, *21*, 22
Pasteurization, 20
Peach skin, *59*
Penicillium, 95
Permanent slides, 30–32
Pins and needles, 47

Plants, looking at, 49–61. *See also specific plants*
Pollen grains, 56, *57*, *58*
Polyester fibers, 45
Pond water, life in, 77–81
Potato starch grains, 54, *55*
Protozoa, 16, 20, 77–81

Rabies vaccine, 22
Razor blade, 46
Rotifer, 80
Royal Society of London, 16

Safety, 31
Salt crystals, 39–40
Sand crystals, 40, *42*
Schleiden, Matthias, 19–20
Schwann, Theodor, 20
Scientific supply companies, 99–101
Silk fibers, 44–45
Slide box, building a, 32, *33*
Slides, making, 28–32
Snowflakes, 45–46
Spirogyra, 78, 85, *86*, 87
Spirostomum, 78
Spores, 92, *93*, *94*
Stage, 27, 34, 35
Stage clips, 27, 34
Stains, 52
Starch grains, 54–56
Substage lamp, 28
Sugar crystals, 40
Sunlight, 34

Teeth, bacteria on, 95–97
Temporary slides, 28–30
Textile fibers, 41–45
Tuberculosis, 20
Typhoid fever, 20

Using the microscope, 32–37

Vaccines, 22
Vacuole, 84, 85, 91
Veins, 73
Viruses, 22, 23
Voluntary muscles, 68, *69*
Vorticella, 78

Water flea, *88*–90
Wool fibers, 44

Yeast, 90, *91*, 92
Yogurt, bacteria in, 97

ABOUT THE AUTHOR

Maurice Bleifeld is Principal Emeritus of Martin Van Buren High School in Queens Village, in New York City. He has won several awards from the National Science Teachers Association, including the Citation for Dedicated Service to Science Education. He was formerly a biology teacher at the Bronx High School of Science in New York City; chairman of the Biology Department at Newtown High School, in Elmhurst, New York City; and president of the New York Biology Teachers Association. He contributed to the classic *Hunting with the Microscope* and wrote *How to Prepare for the College Board Achievement Test in Biology*.